Dealing With Darkness

Jakob Barrientos

DEDICATION

To Leah. My wife, my best friend, and my helpmate.

CONTENTS

Jakob Barrientos

1 MY STORY

I had already been saved for a while when I began to hear about deliverance ministry. I was a "church kid" that knew right from wrong, but I was also very rebellious. I didn't grow up in a church that talked about spiritual activity, so I never learned about the demonic. I wish I would have known more about it sooner.

I started to walk down a very rebellious path at a young age. Drugs, alcohol, sexual immorality, demonic music, and dabbling in witchcraft were a part of my lifestyle. Honestly, if you name it, I have probably done it. My life went on pretty easy for a while. Sin was enjoyable. Even the Bible acknowledges that sin is pleasurable for a season (Heb. 11:25), but in the end, sin results in destruction. I knew that God had a call on my life from a very young age but I simply didn't want it. I thought, "Maybe someday after I've had my fun, I'll get right with God."

It was a few years into my drug use, and by this time, I was a daily pot-smoker. Over the course of a few months, I went from having a great time in sin to experiencing the destruction of it. I was expelled from school, lost my job, got a DUI, lost my girlfriend, and watched many of my friends abandon me in my time of need. I had been in the habit of partying nearly every night when I got off work. I'd willingly engage in stupid acts of rebellion and vandalism. Mostly, my main problem was my drug use. I would use just about anything I could get my sinful hands on including, mushrooms, LSD, and opium. Aside from pot, most of those drugs were not used often until I was introduced to cocaine. Much of the cocaine in Illinois, where I grew up, is laced with crystal methamphetamine.

Within a few short months of being introduced to this wicked drug, I was a full-blown addict. I began losing weight, losing sleep, and snorting several thousands of dollars of my savings up my nose. My tolerance had been growing and I was pushing the limits of how much coke I could do in one setting. I will never forget the time I was sitting in my car alone one night after work. None of my friends were off work yet so I figured I would get an early start. I popped in my Eric Clapton cassette tape and started listening to his song *Cocaine* (I thought I was so cool). That night I did more cocaine than I had ever done in the past. I remember my heart started racing to frightening levels but I thought I'd be okay. Cocaine makes you urinate often and I was experiencing that side effect. I decided to snort one last fat line before I got out of my car to relieve myself. I opened the door to get out of my vehicle and my world was quickly shattered.

I cannot describe what I felt as I began to overdose on drugs. My senses were distorted. Everything I heard sounded metallic or robotic. My vision was blurred and came in what seemed to be a slideshow. I was having flashes of myself standing. Time would pass, and another slide came and I was on the ground. Another slide flashed and I was vomiting. One last slide came across my eyes and I was laying in a pool of my own vomit. There were few logical thoughts that I can remember, but I recall distinctly thinking, "This is it. I'm going to die now." I remember crying out for God to help me (I'm not sure if it was audible or in my mind). I remember, as I laid there in the parking lot in my own vomit, the soothing, healing presence of the Holy Spirit came upon me. I was raised up and immediately sobered. I kicked the coke habit that very night!

I wish I could say that I received salvation that night. Unfortunately, I was still foul, still listening to the satanic music, and still smoked pot on a regular basis, but God had started working in me! It was not too long after my overdose and my encounter with God that I had another encounter. This time it was with the police. I was arrested on drug charges. That night, July 6th, 2004, after I had been bailed out of jail, I gave my life 100% to Jesus. I was not in a revival service or in a prayer meeting. I was sitting on my bed in a place of brokenness and humiliation. It was only then that I truly repented of my sin. Repentance is much more than feeling sorry about your sin. Judas felt remorse over his betrayal of Christ, but Judas never repented. To repent is to turn away from your sin and move in the other direction. Beyond that, true repentance requires a change of mind. We must acknowledge that our actions are sinful and will lead to eternal destruction. We must make up our minds that we will not continue down that path any longer. On that night in July, I changed my mind about the sin that I had been living in. I made a firm decision not to participate in those activities again.

Within the year, I was at Christ for the Nations Institute (CFNI) in Dallas, Texas. I was so hungry for God. I remember the first worship services and feeling the presence of the Holy Spirit in a greater way than I had ever before. I met great, godly friends and I loved to worship, pray, and receive prayer at the altars any chance I could get. It was the second week of school and a man of God named Dr. Carroll Thompson, who had helped in founding CFNI, preached on deliverance. He began talking about demonic oppression, generational curses, and soul-ties. I had heard very little teaching on these subjects until then. Dr. Thompson preached on open doors. He talked about drug addiction and sexual perversion and how we open doors for the enemy to influence us through our sin. He preached repentance, forgiveness, and something that was totally new to me, freedom from sin!

I walked down to that altar as someone who hadn't been in blatant sin for months. I hadn't touched drugs, alcohol, or pornography. I had cleaned up my language and had even thrown out most of my secular CDs. Trust me when I say that I did not go into that service, especially knowing that it was supposed to be about casting out demons, thinking I would have to get prayer. I remember something tugged at my heart to get down to the altar that night. I remember it was like God did a deeper cleaning than I knew was possible. I remember opening my eyes after receiving prayer and it was like the world was brighter and clearer. I didn't have this filter of sin that was constantly before me. I remember the vulgar music that used to continually run through my head had stopped. I remember the lustful way I used to look at women ceased. God did away with things that I thought were simply "normal" thought processes. I remember the very temptation to go back to the comfort of substance abuse was completely wiped away and has never returned to this day. Remember, I was saved before all of this! I was forgiven and was not living in blatant sin, but I was not free. Continually plagued with temptation, I was under attack from the devil when I didn't need to be!

Over the next few nights, I remember walking into the auditorium at CFNI. I didn't care what the topic of the altar call was. I was getting prayer. Generational curses, "better get prayer for that!" Fatherlessness, "I come from a divorced family, so I better get prayer for that!" Ungodly soul ties, "sure!" Homosexuality, "Hmm, I've never struggled with that. Better get prayer just to be safe!" God did such a deep work in me over that week! I was set free from the power of sin and the devil! Ever since that time, I have wanted nothing more than to share that freedom with everyone that I can.

My first semester at CFNI was about to end. One day in prayer, God gave me an open vision. In this vision, I saw a friend who was backslidden. He was standing before me and was a little dirty but nothing looked terribly out of order. I watched as he was split down the middle from the top of his head right down the middle of his body. A shell began to peel off of him and at the same time blood began to pour over him. After the blood stopped flowing, I saw a clean, new person. It was the same friend, but totally new. I knew God was speaking to me. My friend was going to be saved and delivered. I took some time and received council, shared the vision with prophetic and mature counselors, and received their prayers and support.

I went home that summer and convinced this young man to come to a prayer meeting with me. This was a church prayer meeting that had another leader over it. I was shocked when the prayer leader chose other individuals to pray with my friend and wouldn't even let me in the room. I knew by the vision and the confirmation I had received that I was supposed to pray for him and that he would be saved and delivered. Nevertheless, I submitted without complaint. Nothing significant happened that night. In fact, that young man fought with his parents that week, ended up leaving the home, wouldn't return phone calls, was arrested, and ended up in jail. Still, I didn't get upset or speak against the prayer leader even though I certainly thought it was his fault for not letting me pray.

God was faithful. I was submissive and obedient to leadership. The next week, in a miraculous turn of events, that young man ended up in the prayer meeting again. This time, I was allowed to pray. Several others were present for accountability purposes including the prayer leader. They all took turns praying for my friend. Someone else prayed for him and led him in a prayer of repentance. Then the prayer leader turned to me and said I could pray for him. I will never forget what happened next. The young man was sitting in a chair directly across from me. I laid my hand on his leg and said two words, "Dear Lord." Before I could even utter another word, my friend began to manifest demons. His face flooded a shade of green, hatred filled his eyes, and a voice that was not his own began speaking through him. After about an hour of intensive prayer, warring in the spirit, and having this devil cuss me and slap my Bible out of my hand, we found that the root was fatherlessness that had opened the door for bitterness and the oppression of the devil to come in. As we prayed and he repented, we watched as my friend was totally set free from the clutches of the devil! This young man still serves with me in my ministry to this day.

It has been nearly 10 years that I have been moving in deliverance ministry. I have seen manifestations, and better yet, freedom brought into the lives of many believers and unbelievers. Maybe you are reading this and you feel that you are oppressed by the devil. Maybe you are saved but are not walking in the freedom that Christ has for you. You may be reading this in order to equip yourself for deliverance ministry. Whatever reason that you decided to pick up this book, I pray that you will find it to be a blessing and that you will be encouraged and empowered by the chapters to come.

2 THE DIVIDED KINGDOM

We have already demonstrated that there are two different kingdoms in operation today. First, there is the kingdom of Satan which has been well established for many, many years. This is the kingdom that was put in place on the earth at the fall of man. Satan's kingdom will be in existence until the second coming of Christ. Second, we have the kingdom of God that is currently advancing through the redeemed Christians today. These kingdoms are completely contrary and are warring against one another. This may all seem very obvious to you, but what many people fail to recognize is that these contrary kingdoms can operate in the lives of Christians. This includes those who have been saved, filled with the Holy Ghost, and love the Lord. How can you know if Satan's kingdom is operating in or through you?

There is a part of you that earnestly loves Jesus. You want to be used by Him. There's a desire to want to know Him in a deeper and more intimate way. You love the church. You genuinely care for and love people, but there are other passions that operate in you as well. You are bound in sin. There's a propensity in you toward wickedness. You may find that you love some people, but have deep resentment, bitterness, or even hatred for certain individuals. You want to be used by God, but your heart is divided. You have earthly pursuits that are of higher priority. There is a double life going on.

You love the Lord and you love your wife, but when you're alone at night and there is nobody awake or watching, a desire and love for pornography reveals itself. You love Jesus and you love your husband, but he doesn't fulfill your emotional needs. Instead, you turn to your love for your *Fifty Shades of Grey* books. You love God, but that fades when you get around certain friends. Suddenly, drinking, cussing, and smoking do not seem all that bad. You praise Jesus in the church, but your lips gossip, slander, and lie when you get around your girlfriends.

When you walk away from these situations, you often feel the conviction of the Holy Spirit. There is a guilt that grips you because you know your heart is divided. This should not be so! It starts to become clear why the world has marked Christians as hypocrites. Many are in these sin cycles that I have been describing. This is a major area of the ministry of deliverance that Jesus desires to release in the church and in your life today! Prayerfully, we will see an end to this double-minded, divided-kingdom mentality and see freedom released!

In the coming chapters, we will look at the various ways Satan gains access in our lives. We will address generational curses, the bruises of Satan, and other ways we can open the doors to demonic forces. There is no question, the number one way the devil is granted access into our lives is through sin. Before we get too deep into any of this, I want to make a few things clear. When I say we can "open doors" through sin, what does that actually mean?

> Luke 17:20-21 (NKJV)
> "The kingdom of God does not come with observation; nor will they say, 'See here!' or 'See there!' For indeed, the kingdom of God is within you."

> Matthew 12:43-44 (NKJV)
> "When an unclean spirit goes out of a man, he goes through dry places, seeking rest, and finds none. Then he says, 'I will return to my house from which I came.' And when he comes, he finds it empty, swept, and put in order."

We see that Jesus taught that we could have the kingdom of God within us. When we received Jesus as Lord and Savior and received the promised Holy Spirit in our lives, this became a reality. Jesus also taught about how demons can operate in men. These unclean spirits go out of men and will eventually return to what the demon calls "my house." That's the men they came from!

It sounds like we have the capacity for the Holy Spirit and His kingdom to be in and operate through us or for unclean, demonic spirits to be in and operate through us. You can literally serve as a host to the kingdom of God or the kingdom of Satan. To clarify, I am not suggesting that if you have divided passions, or even if you know you have open doors to sin, that you are demon possessed. I have known many Christians who continue to walk in bondage in their life because they assume, "Since I'm a born again Christian, surely I can't have demonic struggles." Having open doors, bondage, or oppression is not necessarily the same as being "demon possessed."

DEMON IN THE HOUSE

The Bible talks about several relationships that demons can have with a human vessel. First is to have a demon. This is demonic possession. There are demons inside of you that can take control and influence your soul (mind, will, and emotions) and even take control of your physical body. Most theologians would say (and I would tend to agree) that an individual that is completely demon possessed has not been born again. Ultimately, this person needs to be delivered, saved, and filled with the Holy Ghost. Second is to be with a demon. This is demonic oppression. This is a demon that is not "in" you, but "on" or "around" you. This is where many individuals are. Demons have been given the right to speak, tempt, lure, and influence individuals. The third is to be demonized. This may be the most unfamiliar to you, but is actually the most frequently used in scripture. Demonized simply speaks of different levels of control. Like I said, we open the door for the devil to influence us through participating in sin. Does this mean the demon has moved into the house? Maybe not completely, but the devil has a foot in the door. It is in this place that the enemy can whisper into your heart, tempting, luring, and drawing you back to the sin that gave him access. The more you open the door to sin, the more influence you give him to speak into your life. This is demonized, not necessarily possessed. Permission has been given to the enemy to oppress. I do not believe there is a clear cut time when you go from oppressed to possessed. It's not like you are only oppressed if you steal 999 times, but if you steal 1,000 times the spirit of kleptomania will possess you. What I can say, however, is that every time you sin, you give more place to the devil. This needs to be taken very seriously.

On one occasion, I was in a church and was in the middle of the transitional prayer time. The worship team had been singing about the blood of Jesus and there was a strong presence in the sanctuary. As I stepped on the stage, I encouraged the church to continue to worship and sing about the blood. All of the sudden, a young man sitting toward the back of the sanctuary began to manifest demons. He was convulsing on the ground as demonic powers seized his physical body. God ministered to that young man and we saw freedom come into his life that very night. The story doesn't end there. Something else happened when that young man manifested demons that was equally powerful. Another young man in the church that night was sitting on the opposite side of the room. As soon as he saw this guy flip out, he ran down to the altar and began repenting of his own sin. The young man at the altars knew about opening doors to the demonic. He later shared with me that he had been living in secret sin. There was always a conviction present and he knew there was a level of oppression in his life. When he saw that demonic manifestation, it was as if he saw for the first time that his sin was giving ground to the devil to influence him. He wanted no more ground to be given to Satan. He repented, confessed, and I prayed with him to receive deliverance. This is why the Bible says in Ephesians to give no place to the devil! To shed a little light on this verse, let us look at a couple of translations:

Ephesians 4:27 (NIV)
"Do not give the devil a foothold"

Ephesians 4:27 (AMP)
"Leave no [such] room or foothold for the devil [give no opportunity to him]."

Place is defined in the Greek language as *Topos* meaning: Place, any portion or space marked off, as it were from surrounding space. An inhabited place, as a city, village, or district.

Another translation is *metaph* meaning: Opportunity, power, occasion for acting.

Topos speaks not only of opening a door, giving a foothold, or giving room to the devil, but also of giving him opportunity, power, and the ability to act in your life. Sin is the avenue in which the devil gains access. You can see why Paul strongly encouraged us to give no place *(topos)* to the devil! If we are going to be responsible believers, we cannot blame the devil for sin that we yield to in carnal disobedience.

Charles Swindoll tells a parable of a certain man who wanted to sell his house in Haiti for $2,000. Another man wanted to buy it but because he was poor, he wasn't able to afford the full price. After much bargaining, the owner agreed to sell the house for half the original price with just one stipulation. That one stipulation would allow him to retain ownership of one small nail protruding slightly over the door. After several years, the original owner wanted the house back but the new owner was unwilling to sell. Disgruntled, the previous owner went to the grocery store and purchased two pounds of hog meat. He proceeded to knock on the door again. He was refused entrance but he produced the title deed and legal ownership rights to the small nail over the door. He demandingly said, "You have to let me in the door because that nail belongs to me!" He quickly gained entrance and proceeded to hang the slab of flesh on the nail over the door. He left saying, "Don't touch my possession or I'll sue you!" Soon the house became unlivable due to the stinking and rotting flesh. The family was forced to sell the house back to the owner of the nail.

The moral of the story is clear. If you allow the devil even one place or nail in your life, he will hang his rotten flesh on it. Eventually that will make your house unfit for Christ's habitation. So how do we get rid of the nails in our kingdom? How can we get rid of this double-minded mentality? Here is a principle to remember. What you submit to will grow stronger, and what you resist will grow weaker.

James 4:7 (NKJV) says,
"Therefore submit to God. Resist the devil and he will flee from you."

Sounds simple enough, right? So what about all the times that you rebuke the devil and he doesn't seem to "buke?" If you have given place to the devil, he doesn't have to leave. He has a right to be there. When you disobey God and continue in sin, you are giving ownership to the devil. This is why every part of our lives, emotions, language, sexuality, etc. needs to be submitted to the lordship (ownership) of Jesus Christ. The devil operates by spiritual law. The devil is very legalistic. If you have allowed sin in your life, he will continue to tempt you and draw you back to those things all day long. The more you submit to him, the greater authority he will have in your life. The first step is repentance! In the coming chapters we will take a deeper look at some practical steps to walking in freedom.

THE DOUBLE MINDED MAN

By now you can begin to see how people become divided. Your heart has been given to the Lord, but through sin, Satan has placed his nails. He has been given a place in our lives and there is a warring between sin and righteousness. This is the divided-kingdom. James speaks of this sort of division. Quite literally, we have a mind for Jesus. You seek wisdom, have faith, and are open to receive from God, but you are divided. There is also a place that is filled with doubt. You are unbelieving and are tossed around like a wave of the sea. James describes the double-minded man.

James 1:6-8 (NKJV)
"But let him ask in faith, with no doubting, for he who doubts is like a wave of the sea driven and tossed by the wind. For let not that man suppose that he will receive anything from the Lord; he is a double-minded man, unstable in all his ways."

I know that some reading this relate to the words that I have shared so far. The words of James are very telling of your heart and mind. Jesus spoke of the same division when addressing the Pharisees about the powers of God verses Satan.

Matthew 12:25 (NKJV)
"Every kingdom divided against itself is brought to desolation, and every city or house divided against itself will not stand."

Jesus warned about divided passions and interests in Luke 9:62 when He said, "If you put your hand to the plow and look back, you're not fit for the kingdom of God (Luke 9:62)." One of these kingdoms are going to win out friend! Either God is going to be victorious in your life and you will see the kingdom of Satan crumble, or there will be a time when the conviction of the Holy Spirit stops and the kingdom of God is no longer found in you. I speak from my own personal experience. I know how exhausting it is to have this divided-kingdom in your life! There is freedom! God can restore!

I have known individuals who do not feel like they need to deal with sin that can lead to demonic influence or live up to a high level of righteousness because they do not preach, are not pursuing full time ministry, and they do not "pour out" on a regular basis. The thing about this divided-kingdom/double-minded state is that it doesn't affect your ability to pour out. We have unfortunately seen many men and women who are used by God and pour out even though they have hidden sin and demonic strongholds. Look again at what James said about the double-minded man:

James 1:6-8 (NKJV)
"But let him ask in faith, with no doubting, for he who doubts is like a wave of the sea driven and tossed by the wind. For let not that man suppose that he will receive

anything from the Lord; he is a double-minded man, unstable in all his ways."

This verse says nothing about your ability to pour out or be used by God. Double mindedness affects your ability to receive, not your ability to give! You may wonder why you have a hard time receiving love from someone or why you can't receive from a man or woman of God. You get nothing when you read the Bible. You have been in countless services where people are receiving in mighty ways and you walk away empty and frustrated. If your mind is divided, James said you can expect to receive nothing from the Lord. We need to cut out the sin, allow God to minister to our mind, and step into freedom!

NOT PERFECT... JUST FORGIVEN

Do not let theology words scare you. Justification and sanctification are foundational truths to the Christian walk that we must understand. On July 6, 2004, I gave my heart completely to Jesus. I began going after God and never looked back. This is justification. Justification defined is the act of God whereby humankind is made or accounted just, or free from guilt or penalty of sin. A simple way to remember the definition of justification is "just-if-I'd-never-sinned."

This is a legal declaration. God, once and for all, declares you as free from the penalty of sin. 2nd Corinthians describes it this way in chapter 5 verse 21, "He made Him who knew no sin, to be sin for us, that we might become the righteousness of God in Him" (NKJV). This is what Christians commonly refer to as the great exchange. Jesus took our sin and gave us His righteousness. When the Father looks at us, He sees His Son and His righteousness. When the Father looked upon Jesus on the cross, He saw and accounted our sin to Him. Powerful! Now would be a good time to say "Thank you, Jesus!"

This is our position. Spiritually, the work has been done. Jesus has died. He has given us His righteousness. It is a done work. Justified! Beyond our position, we need to consider our condition. Are we as perfect today as Jesus? Are you walking 100% in the righteousness of God in Christ? Unfortunately, no. This is where the second part of salvation comes in, sanctification.

Sanctification defined is to make holy; set apart as sacred, consecrate, to purify, free from sin.

Sanctification is God taking us from our present condition and into our spiritual position. Notice the definition of justification. It frees us from the guilt or penalty of sin. Sanctification makes us actually free from sin, not just from the guilt and penalty that comes along with it. Justification positions us in Jesus Christ's holiness. Sanctification actually makes us holy! The pursuit of holiness through sanctification needs to be the goal of all Christians today!

Hebrews 12:14 (NKJV)
"Pursue peace with all people, and holiness, without which no one will see the Lord."

The word holiness means to be bright, clean, new, fresh, and untarnished. This is to be our pursuit, and not only that, but this is what God wants to make you! That is the sanctifying ministry of the Holy Spirit.

1st Peter 2:24 (NKJV)
"Who Himself bore our sins in His own body on the tree, that we, having died to sins, might live for righteousness."

Not only does God want us to become the righteousness of God in Christ, but also, he bore our sins on the cross so that we could die to our sin and live and walk as righteous men and women of God. None of this "I'm not perfect, just forgiven" junk. I have seen bumper stickers and t-shirts that have that statement and I believe it sends a terrible message to the world. This is the message that the "I'm not perfect, just forgiven" statement implies. Let's say you have two guys, Sinner Sam and Pharisaical Phil. Sinner Sam is a wife beating, adulterating, drunk that cheats on his taxes and steals money from his work place. Pretty bad, huh? Then you have Pharisaical Phil, who is also a wife beating, adulterating, drunk that cheats on his taxes and steals money from his work place. Guess what? Phil goes to church. He has been baptized, so when he dies, he gets to go to heaven. Poor wretched, heathen Sam doesn't go to church, so he has to go to hell.

Obviously, this is an extreme example, but this is how many believe salvation works! Our spiritual position changes since we believe in Jesus but our lives do not change due to the belief that we will never be perfect. This is a lie from the pit of hell. Do not accept any of this "I'm not perfect, just forgiven", damnable doctrine! Truth be told, both Sinner Sam and Pharisaical Phil are going to hell! In fact, Phil, who has heard the truth and remains unchanged, will be in a hotter ring of hell (if there is such a thing) because he should have known better.

SAVED FROM (NOT IN) SIN

Matthew 1:21 (NKJV)
"And she will bring forth a Son, and you shall call His name Jesus, for He will save His people from their sins."

This was an awesome, prophetic declaration about the ministry of Jesus that came to Joseph by word of an angel. There is a big difference between being saved in your sin and saved from your sin! Scripture says, "He will save his people from their sins." Do you know what the Greek word "from" actually translates to? It translates to "from." There is no possibility of it being mixed up with the word "in." Meaning, if you stay in the sin from which Jesus came to save you, I would seriously question your salvation. The best-case scenario is you have a double minded, divided kingdom happening, but even at that, you are walking on shaky ground, unstable in your ways, and unable to receive. Surely we do not want to continue in that state! Sanctification means freedom from sin! Deliverance from sin! Look at these verses and pray them over your life. This is the will of God for your life:

I Thessalonians 4:3-4 (NKJV)
"For this is the will of God, your sanctification: that you should abstain from sexual immorality; that each of you should know how to possess his own vessel in sanctification and honor,"

I Thessalonians 5:23-24 (NKJV)
"Now may the God of peace Himself sanctify you completely; and may your whole spirit, soul, and body be preserved blameless at the coming of our Lord Jesus Christ. He who calls you is faithful, who also will do it."

God will sanctify you completely, spirit, soul, and body! We know our spirit is alive in Christ. That happens when you are justified. Have you submitted your soul, mind, will and your emotions to God? Do you still sin with your body or are you blameless? I'm not talking about sinless perfection. I'm not saying, "I can't sin", but God has given me freedom from sin! Now I can say "I don't have to sin!" We were once unredeemed sinners that were subject to the flesh and whatever demonic powers we gave place to. Now we are redeemed, cleansed, and being sanctified. Now we have the ability to not sin. We are free!

Galatians 5:1 (NKJV)
"Stand fast therefore in the liberty by which Christ has made us free, and do not be entangled again with a yoke of bondage."

Romans 8:1-2 (NKJV)
"There is therefore now no condemnation to those who are in Christ Jesus, who do not walk according to the flesh, but according to the Spirit. For the law of the Spirit of life in Christ Jesus has made me free from the law of sin and death."

It's time to cut the sin and the junk out of our lives! It's time to repent (to turn away from sin) and change your mind about what you have been okay with in the past! It's time to leave the world and its corruption!

2nd Corinthians 6:14 (NKJV)
"Do not be unequally yoked together with unbelievers. For what fellowship has righteousness with lawlessness? And what communion has light with darkness? Or what part has a believer with an unbeliever? For you are the temple of the living God. As God has said: I will dwell in them and walk among them. I will be their God, and they shall be My people."

Do you want to be a kingdom and a temple of the Holy Spirit, or a divided kingdom with divided passions and a divided mind? We need to consider the question that is posed here. What part or what fellowship should we have with the world, sin, corruption, and even unbelievers? Paul said do not be unequally yoked with unbelievers. This is not talking about not having friends or a spouse that are not as "on fire" as you. This is talking about your fellowship with unbelievers and with the world. Now I already know the question is rattling in your brain, "How can I influence my bad friends if I'm not around them?" The fact of the matter is you need to get free and clean before you need to start worrying about the sinners around you. If they are willing to seek healing and pursue God alongside you, great! The Bible is pretty clear about what keeping bad company will lead to.

1st Corinthians 15:33-34 (AMP)
"Do not be deceived and misled! Bad company [evil companionship, ungodly influence, rebellious spirits]

corrupts good morals [good habits, depraves good manners, morals, and godly character]. Awake to righteousness and do not sin; for some do not have the knowledge of God. I speak this to your shame."

Bad company is like putting on a white pair of gloves. If you were to take up a handful of mud, your gloves would get muddy, right? Notice the mud does not get "glovey." The clean glove gets contaminated by the mud, not vice versa. That same chapter of Corinthians goes on to say this:

1st Corinthians 15:50 (NKJV)
"Corruption cannot inherit incorruption."

This means your goodness will not rub off on a bad person. This is why the Bible gives us instruction.

2nd Corinthians 6:17-18 (NKJV)
"Come out from among them and be separate, says the Lord. Do not touch what is unclean, and I will receive you. I will be a Father to you, and you shall be My sons and daughters, says the Lord."

It is true that Jesus was around sinners, but don't believe for an instant that Jesus was around people that were actively living in adultery, drunkenness, and the like. When sinners would come to Jesus, He would cast the devil out of them, forgive them, and encourage them to go and sin no more.

I remember when I was in the valley of decision and was deciding whether or not to give my life to Jesus. I was concerned about my lost friends. Truth be told, the devil was still looking for a way to keep me in sin and I was still wrestling with total surrender to Jesus. I am glad I resisted the devil on that one. I almost decided not to turn to Jesus for the sake of a few friends and the positive impact that I might have on them. I chose to leave that lifestyle and pursue Jesus with everything. Many of my friends went their own way. There are a few that eventually received salvation and some that even serve alongside me today.

To date, I have had the privilege of pastoring a rapidly growing congregation that has seen many saved, healed, and delivered. I have seen sinners come in, get turned around, and then go off to Bible College as they pursue the call of God on their lives. I have been blessed to preach overseas, speak in churches around the world, plant churches, and hold crusades. Best of all, I know my eternity is in Heaven. God's plan for your life is so much bigger than what you could possibly fathom. Do not forsake the high call of God because you are unwilling to come out from among your lost friends and be separate. Don't run from the call of God because the church, as you see it, is full of hypocrites.

On that note, I want to break the mentality that the church is full of hypocrites. The only way we will do that is if we walk in the freedom that Jesus has made available! No more mixture! We are called to be separate! A spiritual father in my life made a statement that has stuck with me from the first time I heard it. As an individual who is believing for a mighty outpouring of the Spirit of God on this end time generation, I have made this a goal and life mission.

"The church without mixture will have the Holy Spirit without measure"
- Dr. Carroll Thompson

Whether you are believing for the power of the Holy Ghost in your life, in your church, or have a vision for a world-wide revival, it will not begin until you cut out sin and mixture and persistently pursue God and His holiness.

FEAR NOT!

2nd Timothy 1:7 (NKJV)
"For God has not given us a spirit of fear, but of power and of love and of a sound mind."

Did you know that the phrase "Fear Not" is the most repeated phrase in the Bible? I know that all this talk of demons could frighten some. Maybe you have already seen or encountered demonic forces and are reading this book seeking freedom from the enemy. I would echo the command of God over your life, "Fear not!"

If you have come to Christ then you do not need to fear the devil. I want you to fear God who will bring judgment if you have not repented of your sin. Take some time and read the Bible. Generally speaking, Hollywood has painted demons as powerful, terrifying figures, while angels on the other hand are seen as chubby, harp-playing babies. This could not be more backwards! Have you ever noticed in the Bible that nearly every angelic visitation begins with these awesome figures speaking the words "fear not" before they spoke anything more? People would see these angelic beings and be inclined to worship them, fall to the ground as dead, or run away terrified. Angels would quickly calm them. Imagine if you had seen an angel. The Bible describes them as huge soldiers with fiery swords and some with six wings. The word "Seraphim" (a type of angel) literally means "the burning ones." This description of these hulking angels that are covered in fire sounds more like man's depiction of demons. Now do you understand why they would say, "fear not?"

Demons, on the other hand, are a very different story. Every time they had an encounter with Jesus, they were screaming, crying out, and begging not to be cast out. They are puny and weak. They knew they had no authority over Jesus. You may say "Of course those demons were scared, Jakob! They were dealing with Jesus!" It's true, but remember our position in Christ. If you have been redeemed and are now seated with Christ in heavenly places, you also have authority over the enemy!

I will never forget one night we were having an all night prayer meeting in a church that I served in as the senior pastor. We were taking time to pray through every room in the church and lift up the ministries that took place in them. I was in the sound booth praying for the media ministry when from somewhere else in the church I heard a loud "GAAAHHHH!" I looked around at some of the others in the sound booth to see if they had heard this blood-curdling scream, and sure enough, they had. Before I had a chance to say or ask anything we heard another scream. All of the sudden a young man burst through my door and said, "Pastor, we were praying in your office and this guy started screaming and shaking. I think he's manifesting demons!" I rushed down the stairs through the hall to my office and noticed a few people in there. Right in the middle of the room curled in a fetal position was a middle-aged man shaking, sweating, and periodically screaming. As this man was met with the presence of the Holy Spirit those demonic powers began to swell up in fear. That demon knew that his time was short. I encouraged those in the room to begin to pray in the Spirit and to plead the blood of Jesus. I laid hands on the man, and within minutes, we saw complete freedom come upon him.

You do not need to fear. In fact, if you receive freedom and begin to walk in the righteousness of God in Christ, the devil will be the one that has to fear. Christ has overcome! Now before you decide you are ready to start a deliverance ministry, make sure you check out the section "Who in Hell Knows Your Name."

Preface

I would like to say before you dive into the next few sections that there is controversy around some of the topics that I'm touching on in this book. Throughout the coming chapters I will deal with soul ties, generational curses, and even share some thoughts about homosexuality. However, I do realize that not everyone will agree with me on the topic of generational curses. Others believe, but they feel there is too strong of an emphasis placed on this concept. I pray you will read and study the next few chapters with an open heart. This book was birthed from my own years of ministry and experience in dealing with darkness. Beyond this, you will see that I always refer back to what the Bible has to say. I would like to mention that while I touch on generational curses, there is also a heavy emphasis on generational blessings, a topic I have rarely heard teaching on.

At the end of the day, agree or disagree, my desire is to see you, the reader, walking in the freedom that God has for you. I want to see you fully equipped to share that freedom with others. Embrace the blessings that God has in store for your life

3 BEHIND DOOR NUMBER TWO

Now that we see some of the damages of sin and the primary way the enemy is given authority in our lives, it's time to look at some of the other major ways that he is granted access. Another way Satan is given an open door into our lives is through generational curses. Ultimately, the root of all open doors and oppression is sin, but the Bible speaks about times that the sins of the father are passed on to children.

Numbers 14:18 (NKJV)
"The Lord is longsuffering and abundant in mercy, forgiving iniquity and transgression; but He by no means clears the guilty, visiting the iniquity of the fathers on the children to the third and fourth generation."

Exodus 20:5 (NKJV)
"You shall not bow down to them nor serve them. For I, the Lord your God, am a jealous God, visiting the iniquity of the fathers upon the children to the third and fourth generations of those who hate Me,"

Iniquity is more than sin. The simplest definition I have heard is that iniquity is repeated sin. I am not talking about a one-time stumbling into sin. Blatant repeated sin (years of alcoholism, sexual immorality, abuse, and outbursts of anger) can open the door for those sins to be transferred or passed onto the children up to the third and fourth generation.

Consider David, God used him mightily in delivering Israel from the hand of the Philistines and the strongman, Goliath. God referred to David as "a man after His own heart." It was this same David who committed adultery and murder. I would not say David was demon possessed, but he was certainly under demonic influence. Even though God forgave David when he repented one year later, the demonic seed that was sown affected his family in a horrible way. One of his sons died immediately as an infant. One of David's older sons raped his daughter, which resulted in another one of his sons seeking revenge and ultimately killing the brother who committed the rape. Two of David's sons tried to kill him and take his kingdom out from under him. Another son slept with David's wives. Solomon, who was also David's son, became king and was a womanizing, idol worshipper. Sin brings a curse. Nathan prophesied to David in 2nd Samuel 12:10, "The sword shall never depart from your house". Solomon affirmed this curse when he wrote in Proverbs 26:2, "A curse causeless shall not come".

If you are anything like me, you are probably already racking your brain. "I have a lot of sin in my family. Are you saying this will be passed on?" If that sin goes unrepented of and the curse remains unbroken, it's very possible. Here is a strong point of encouragement for you. Even though

Solomon and David's other sons suffered and were born into sin and bondage because of their father's sins, there was another descendant in David's bloodline. That descendant is redemption embodied, Jesus Christ!

Generational curses are real, but through repentance and the shed blood of Jesus, there is deliverance. You do not need to be bound by anger because your daddy and your grandpa were angry. You do not need to walk under the oppression of anxiety or depression because your momma and your grandma did. It doesn't matter if your family line has seen generations where young girls get pregnant out of wedlock. The ministry of Jesus is about breaking generational curses!

There have been some studies done that affirm the reality of generational curses. A few years ago, a study was done called "COGA - the Collaborative Study on the Genetics of Alcoholism." They found that nearly 40% of alcoholism is passed from generation to generation through genes. Before I continue, I would say it's not a genetic issue as much as it is a spiritual issue, but I want you to know what these scientists and psychologists have to say. The study revealed the following:

• A child of a alcohol dependent parent is 4-9 times more likely to develop the same problems.

• 95% of alcoholics have immediate family members with the same drinking problem.

• Nearly ¼ of children of alcoholics become alcohol dependent themselves.

This expansive study was done over a two year period and concluded in 2012. Part of the focus was on twins and personality types ultimately trying to isolate the "alcoholic" gene. The overwhelming consent was that alcoholism and genetics are linked. They will continue to search for that alcoholic gene, but I personally believe that they won't find it. They will continue to see the same results because it's not linked to genes, but rather a generational curse. What we are seeing are children that have been born into the same bondage that bound their parents.

There are similar studies on so many topics that include: Drug addiction, anxiety, depression, suicides, divorce, homosexuality, abuse, anger, A.D.D., and even medical issues, such as cancer, arthritis, mental disorders, and things like Alzheimer's.

DISCERNING BETWEEN FLESH AND SPIRIT

Hebrews 5:14 speaks about those who have their senses exercised to discern both good and evil. This is very important. I do not believe that all sin is caused by demonic oppression. Carnal flesh is something we wrestle with daily. When dealing with demonic issues, I have seen people go into hyper-spiritual mode where everything is blamed on a demon. Just because you snuck a cigarette when you were 9 years old does not mean you need deliverance. If you get a flat tire, you do not need to cast the spirit of flatness out of your car. I do not believe that all sickness is the devil. Our falling and decaying flesh gets sick at times. You may get cancer and it may or may not be a generational curse.

I struggled with substance abuse and sexual immorality which were found on both sides of my family. Cancer was very prevalent on my father's side of the family, which I have not, and do not want to battle. When I was around ministry for generational curses and heard about sin, sickness, and other things that could affect me through the sins of my parents, I didn't wait. I didn't fast and pray for a month and wait for a prophetic confirmation that my struggles were the result of a generation curse. I saw the trend in my parents and I knew that I had sinned in those areas as well. I knew I didn't want cancer so I responded to the altar call for generational curses.

I would encourage you to do the same. You may respond and find that there was no oppression on you. So what? You got prayer and were blessed. The alternative is much worse. Maybe you choose not to respond or seek prayer to break generational curses because pride or fear holds you back. What if you walk around struggling with a sin issue, a constant nagging oppression, or some emotional scar that God could have broken off or healed in one moment of prayer?

You might be surprised. When I was pastoring, I had a high school student brought to my office. His parents said he was rebellious, constantly in trouble at school, and listened to demonic metal music. The parents didn't bring him to me for deliverance. They didn't believe he was struggling with demons but that he needed some council, some wisdom, and possibly a spiritual father in his life. I agreed to speak with him. In that first meeting, I laid hands on this kid and he manifested demons. There were some strong demonic and generational curses that needed broken. The young man was set free but I remember walking out of that meeting almost finding it humorous. I had intended to have a peaceful 20-minute meeting with a young rebellious teen and it turned into an intensive, hour-long time of deliverance. Word of this demonic manifestation spread through the church and within a week I got a call from a grandmother who wanted to set up a deliverance meeting with her grandson. The grandmother and the parents all swore that their junior high schooler was demon possessed and they even listed the spirits they believed were oppressing him. I spent time in prayer and fasting, asking for discernment. I was feeling like what the family was telling me wasn't on point but maybe I wasn't fully informed. I met with this young man and his father and we talked for a bit. The young man seemed fairly open to receive. I laid hands on him and prayed as I had been instructed and nothing resulted. No manifestation or significant ministry took place that day. Walking out of the meeting, I shared with the family that I believed the struggle was not with demonic forces, but with the flesh. He needed some discipline, godly boundaries, and some tough love. They didn't care much for that council. I ended up talking with another individual who is involved with deliverance ministry. He asked me how my prayer time with the young man had gone. I shared everything with him including my council to the parents. Come to find out, the family had approached this individual some time earlier with the same requests and he had come to the same conclusion that I had. No demonic struggles. It was very unfortunate. Over the coming years, I watched this man sink more and more into a slump of defeated depression. He kept believing that he was demon possessed, a lie that had been spoken over his life repeatedly. A demonic stronghold was formed because of this lie.

This leads to another topic altogether, strongholds. We talk about a demonic stronghold as if it is a form of possession or oppression, but what does it actually mean in this context? A stronghold is a wrong belief. This young man was not demon possessed, but after he heard it so many times, he believed he was. Years later after he had graduated high school, I had the opportunity to share and pray with him. I believe he was, and still is, under that wrong mentality.

You know what breaks a demonic stronghold? No, not a

powerful prayer time or even the anointing of the Holy Spirit operating through a man or woman of God. The truth breaks strongholds. There is no greater truth than the truth of the Bible. This is why I have included pages at the end of this book, like "Scriptures for Victory", so that you can begin to break off strongholds and walk in the freedom God has made available for us simply by declaring the truth of God's Word over your life!

SOUL TIES

Another major way we see the door opened for demonic oppression is through what is commonly referred to as a "soul tie." While you may think of soul ties as negative, did you know that they can also be positive?

The definition of a soul tie is something (spirit, person, object) that is able to influence your soul (mind, will, emotions) either towards or away from God. Obviously, we want our soul influenced towards God. You will notice that deliverance is always dealing with the soul. We are made up of three parts: Spirit, soul, and body. Our spirit has been redeemed. It is good, it was cleansed, and it is righteous. Our body or flesh is unredeemed. It's inclined towards sinfulness. It is prone to sickness and disease and will eventually die and rot away. In eternity, we will receive glorified bodies that will be as redeemed, whole, and righteous as our spirit is today. The third part is in the middle of the previous two. It is our soul. It is with our mind that we choose to either submit to what the spirit speaks or submit to the lust of the flesh. We choose whether our emotions will be subject to the spirit or to the flesh. There is a natural lust of the flesh, but it is your mind that will choose to either dwell on that or look away (think on pure things and so submit to the spirit). The Holy Spirit's sanctifying work is present to move our soul into alignment with the spirit. Alternately, we have demonic forces that wish to influence our soul to submit to the lust of the flesh. It is in the soul where we will either find victory and freedom or defeat and bondage. This is why understanding soul ties is very important. Take a moment to check your heart and see what or who is influencing your soul either towards or away from God.

There are several types of soul ties:

Soul ties with God:

Deuteronomy 10:20 (AMP)
"You shall [reverently] fear the Lord your God; you shall serve Him and cling to Him, and by His name and presence you shall swear."

Cling or cleave in the Strong's Concordance means to cling or adhere, cleave (fast together), or be joined together. We are to form a soul tie with the Lord. This is very important for us in our daily warfare and deliverance. We must commit ourselves to the Lord and serve Him. As this soul tie is formed, we will be able to say as Jesus said, "I and My Father are One" (John 10:30). We are yoked together in Christ! Soul ties with God are obviously good.

Soul ties with Christians:

Ephesians 4:16 (AMP)
"For because of Him the whole body (the church, in all its various parts), closely joined and firmly knit together by the joints and ligaments with which it is supplied, when each part [with power adapted to its need] is

working properly [in all its functions], grows to full maturity, building itself up in love."

Colossians 2:2 (AMP)
"[For my concern is] that their hearts may be braced (comforted, cheered, and encouraged) as they are knit together..." v. 19) "and not holding fast to the Head, from Whom the entire body, supplied and knit together by means of its joints and ligaments, grows with a growth that is from God."

This speaks greatly of unity! Many times we simply look at the physical aspect of the church. Unity is something that must take place in our soul. As we are "knit together" not only will we be sensitive to the needs of those we are one with, but we will be able to function as one. Soul ties with other Christians are also good to have in your life.

Soul ties with pastors or leaders:

2nd Samuel 20:2
"So all the men of Israel withdrew from David and followed Sheba, son of Bichri: but the men of Judah stayed faithfully with their king, from the Jordan to Jerusalem."

This is a tremendous story. David was a man who knew betrayal but he was also privileged to have men whose hearts and souls were with their king. These were men who would lay down their life for their king. In fact, just a few chapters later in 2nd Samuel 23, David, after a war with his "mighty men of valor", sighs, and in passing says, "Oh, that someone would give me a drink of the water from the well of

Bethlehem, which is by the gate!" It would be no different than if you were thirsty and made a remark about how nice a cold drink would be. Several of David's men heard their honored king's request, took up their swords and fought through the Philistine Army camps. All of that was done just to get to the well and retrieve some of the water. They brought it back to their king who was astonished. Soul ties under the right leadership are good and beneficial. Leaders that are directing you towards God ought to be honored and blessed.

Soul ties with your husband/wife:

Genesis 2:24
"Therefore a man shall leave his father and his mother and shall become united and cleave to his wife, and they shall become one flesh."

Soul ties with your spouse are always good. If your spouse is an unbeliever, you don't need to be concerned about ungodly soul ties. 1st Corinthians 7:14 says, "The believer, because of the blood, sanctifies the unbeliever and the children are sanctified also as holy." This doesn't mean that your spouse is saved. They need to come to repentance as well. Although, you and your household can be effectively covered in the blood and protected even if one part of the house is not saved.

Soul ties with friends:

I Samuel 18:1
"When David had finished speaking to Saul, the soul of Jonathan was knit with the soul of David, and Jonathan

loved him as his own life."

Soul ties with friends can be good or bad. It is important to know who you are allowing to influence your soul. As you come close to your friends, they have the ability to greatly influence your soul for the better or worse. We have already discussed not having fellowship with unbelievers. Make sure your friends are influencing you towards God, not away from Him.

Soul ties in adultery and fornication:

Genesis 34:2-3 (NKJV)
"And when Shechem son of Hamor the Hivite, prince of the country, saw her, he seized her, lay with her, and humbled, defiled, and disgraced her. But his soul longed for and clung to Dinah daughter of Jacob, and he loved the girl and spoke comfortingly to her young heart's wishes."

Proverbs 6:32 (NKJV)
"Whoever commits adultery with a woman lacks understanding; He who does so destroys his own soul."

There is no way around it; soul ties in adultery and fornication are a very bad deal. The word "joined" is used in relation to marriage. In Ephesians 5:31, we are told that a man is to be "JOINED" unto his wife. The literal meaning in Greek is: to cleave, stick to, glue, or cement. Another use of "joined" is found in Matthew 19:6 where we are told concerning marriage: "Therefore what God has joined together, let not man separate." "Joined" can be translated as "yoked together." There is a clear warning against fornication in scripture, "Flee also youthful lusts" (2 Timothy 2:22). The Bible says that one who is "joined to a harlot is one body" (1 Corinthians 6:15).

> 1st Corinthians 6:15 -20 (NKJV)
> "Do you not know that your bodies are members of Christ? Shall I then take the members of Christ and make them members of a harlot? Certainly not! Or do you not know that he who is joined to a harlot is one body with her? For "the two," He says, "shall become one flesh." But he who is joined to the Lord is one spirit with Him. Flee sexual immorality. Every sin that a man does is outside the body, but he who commits sexual immorality sins against his own body. Or do you not know that your body is the temple of the Holy Spirit who is in you, whom you have from God, and you are not your own? For you were bought at a price; therefore glorify God in your body and in your spirit, which are God's."

Paul talks about sexual immorality and why it negatively effects people. You will become joined as "one flesh" (body, soul, and spirit) with him or her. As a consequence, you have now formed an intimate bond or "soul tie" with that person. Sex is an act of all three parts of your body. Through sexual relationships outside of marriage, demonic soul ties can be established. Those who engage in sex outside of marriage become one flesh, which God purposed solely for a husband and wife.

> Ephesians 5:31 (NKJV)
> "For this reason a man shall leave his father and his mother and shall be joined to his wife, and the two shall become one flesh."

IT'S NOT JUST SEX

Have you ever noticed when the Bible speaks about sexual relationships it rarely says "sex." For example, take Adam and Eve. In Genesis 4:1, it does not say that Adam consummated his relationship with Eve or that Adam had sex with Eve. The Bible says, "And Adam knew Eve as his wife, and she became pregnant." God has created a level of fulfillment, encouragement, intimacy, and knowledge that can only be given and received through sexual union. I "know" my wife in a way nobody else will. I not only have an emotional and physical bond with her, but we have been unified in soul and spirit. I affirm who she is and she affirms who I am.

Have you ever noticed in the world that boys are considered "men" when they sleep around? It's as if having sexual relations affirm who a man is. The affirmation he is seeking is something that God has designed to be found in sexual union with your spouse within holy matrimony. There is a godly encouragement that the husband gives the wife and the wife gives the husband. Sex is not "just sex." It's a union that spans spirit, soul, and body.

God has created one man and one woman to be able to relate to one another in this way. They fulfill and affirm who each other are and who God created them to be. Numerous times through scripture, you see that individuals in adultery, fornication, or other sexual sin were punished by death. They would be taken outside of the camp and stoned. The reason for the stoning is not just because they had sex outside of marriage or because they were unfaithful to their spouse. Leviticus 20:12 (NKJV) says, "Both of them shall surely be put to death; they have wrought confusion; their blood shall be upon their own heads."

This is seen repeatedly through Leviticus and once in Exodus. They are put to death because they have created confusion in Israel. Why? The wrong man is telling the wrong woman who she is! If you look in a concordance, you will find that the opposite of knowledge is confusion. Seeking the "knowledge" that can only be had while in the covenant and confines of marriage creates confusion rather than knowledge.

Confusion in the Greek is *Tebel* meaning confusion (violation of nature or divine order) a. perversion (in sexual sin).

1st Corinthians 14:33 (NKJV)
"For God is not the author of confusion but of peace,"

James 3:16 (NKJV)
"For where envy and self-seeking exist, confusion and every evil thing are there."

Notice that James links every evil thing to confusion! Remember the doors that opened to David's children through his sexual sin? I remember hearing the testimony of serial killer Ted Bundy as he was on death row for killing nearly 30 women. Ted shared that his struggles began as a young child when he found a pornographic magazine around a dumpster (open door). This is where oppression came into his life as he gave place to the devil. As that sin grew and he continued to submit to temptations, his lust and perversion grew to seeking real relationships. This eventually led to violent sexual relationships, rape, murder, and even necrophilia. Obviously, this is an extreme example, but it's a real life example of how even the most seemingly small sexual sin opens the door to confusion and every evil thing.

You may wonder why you have security issues or come upon an identity crisis. You may wonder why your heart goes back to relationships from the past even though you are in a loving relationship with your spouse. There is confusion through soul ties. This confusion hinders our ability to receive from God and from His Word! It's linked to every evil thing! Through prayer, generational curses and ungodly soul ties can be broken!

The Bible is so insistent on fleeing sexual immorality! You may be hard-pressed to find verses condemning certain sins. In every list of sin, the Bible is constantly warning about the damages of sexual sin. This is because you open the door for soul ties, demonic oppression, spiritual confusion, double-mindedness, and generational curses that will affect your children and even grandchildren. The secret sin you believe is not hurting anyone is not only opening demonic doors in your life, but is opening doors in the lives of your sons and daughters. David sinned in this area and the door was open for his kids, not just the door for adultery, but every evil thing including: murder, incest, rape, and rebellion. If there is sexual sin in your life, today is your day for forgiveness and freedom.

IS THERE HOPE?

All this talk about generational curses, confusion, and soul ties might seem kind of hopeless. Not so! Earlier we read about generational curses in Numbers.

Numbers 14:18 (NKJV)
"The Lord is longsuffering and abundant in mercy, forgiving iniquity and transgression; but He by no means clears the guilty, visiting the iniquity of the fathers on the children to the third and fourth generation."

Let us take a moment and focus on some of the other portions of this scripture. Is the Lord patient? Is He longsuffering? Is He abundant in mercy? Does He forgive iniquity and transgression? Yes to all of the above! Numbers said He will not clear the guilty, but if you have come to Jesus and His blood has washed you, are you guilty? No! This is where the power of deliverance is! The blood of Jesus! Redemption!

This passage in Numbers was a conversation between Moses and God. Moses went on to pray this:

Numbers 14:19 (NKJV)
"Pardon the iniquity of this people, I pray, according to

the greatness of Your mercy, just as You have forgiven this people, from Egypt even until now."

What did God do for the children of Israel in Egypt? He delivered them! Do you know how our merciful, longsuffering, and forgiving God responds to Moses plea?

Numbers 14:20 (NKJV)
"Then the Lord said: "I have pardoned, according to your word; but truly, as I live, all the earth shall be filled with the glory of the Lord."

Remember the second verse we read about generational curses?

Exodus 20:5-6 (NKJV)
"You shall not bow down to them nor serve them. For I, the Lord your God, am a jealous God, visiting the iniquity of the fathers upon the children to the third and fourth generations of those who hate Me, But showing mercy to thousands, to those who love Me and keep My commandments."

That happened through Jesus and continues to happen today through the ministry of the Holy Spirit! God is delivering, God is forgiving, God is breaking generational curses, and God is pouring out His glory! There is hope!

When talking about generational curses we tend to focus on the bad. I spent the beginning part of this chapter highlighting the reality of soul ties and generational curses. We cannot forget the blessings and the glory! Sin may have power over a few generations, but mercy can touch thousands! Let us address the curses so we can step into the blessings of The Lord!

THE SERPENTS SEED

Isaiah speaks of generational curses and these soul ties using slightly different verbiage:

Isaiah 14:29
"For out of the serpent's seed will come forth a viper, and its offspring will be a fiery flying serpent."

This whole chapter is speaking of the judgment of Satan, the antichrist, demonic oppression, and affliction (serpent's seed). This gives way to generational curses and oppression of the mind (flying serpent). You may not be able to look at the sin cycles in your life and say there is a clear generational curse. We have been looking at how sin can intensify and even change from generation to generation. What was sexual sin in one generation has opened the door for every evil thing in the next.

Tebel not only means confusion and mixture but is also used to describe what is unnatural. The Bible uses tebel to describe incest, homosexuality, and bestiality. Many homosexuals will have the same story, "I was born this way." Similar to the alcohol gene, some have tried to say there is a gay gene. This gene has not been found and I don't believe it will be. It's spiritual, not genetic.

Through our evangelistic efforts we have ministered extensively to the homosexual community. It's amazing how many times you begin to share scripture and they begin to say "I'm confused." There are many highly educated individuals who can wrap their mind around deep topics but when you begin to lay out the simplicity of the gospel, it confuses them (tebel).

Gaining an understanding on generational curses and how people can even be born with certain tendencies can help you to understand why so many believe they were born homosexual. It's important to recognize God did not create them that that way. While a great number of practicing homosexuals could point out an instance of sexual, physical, or verbal abuse that could have opened the door for Satan to afflict (bruises of Satan), there are others who were born with a level of confusion (tebel).

Some homosexuals may have had a mother or father that allowed sexual immorality into their lives. They opened the door for demonic oppression which gave way to a curse upon their child who is now walking in that confusion that we have already outlined. All of our parents have sinned. Every person probably has a tendency towards a certain sin. I was born with a tendency toward addiction, acceptance issues, and sexual immorality. I didn't open the door to it or ask for it. As much as we would like to look at children and think they are sinless and without flaw inside and out, the fact of the matter is, they are not born perfect.

Most are born broken in one area or another. It doesn't take long for us to recognize that some children are born with insecurity, fear, or lying. Most do not have any doctrinal issue acknowledging this, but when it comes to homosexual desire we change our view. The same way I have had natural tendencies toward jealousy and insecurity; there are some that are born carrying an unnatural sexual tendency.

It was not God who made them that way. The seed of the serpent has brought confusion to them but that doesn't make it right. Sin is still sin. God wants to bring healing to that brokenness. He wants to cut off those soul ties and break your generational curses. He wants to completely remove the serpent's seed from your life and your offspring.

From Curses to Blessings

Genesis 22:18 (NKJV)
"In your seed all the nations of the earth shall be blessed, because you have obeyed My voice."

I have shared briefly about the serpent's seed, but did you know that the Bible speaks of another seed? This is the seed in which all nations would be blessed rather than cursed. In Genesis, Abraham received a promise of a blessing to all nations and generations. This promise has stood from Abraham through every generation to Jesus. Galatians 3 talks about how we can receive the blessing of Abraham.

Galatians 3:8-9, 13-14 (NKJV)
"And the Scripture, foreseeing that God would justify the Gentiles by faith, preached the gospel to Abraham beforehand, saying, "In you all the nations shall be blessed." So then those who are of faith are blessed with believing Abraham. ... Christ has redeemed us from the curse of the law, having become a curse for us (for it is written, "Cursed is everyone who hangs on a tree"), that the blessing of Abraham might come upon the Gentiles in Christ Jesus, that we might receive the promise of the Spirit through faith."

The promises of Abraham! It's salvation in Jesus Christ! It's the breaking of curses because Jesus became a curse for us. It's receiving the Holy Ghost! There is so much more! God expands territory, He extends His kingdom through you, blesses you financially, and opens the heavens over your life! The blessings of Abraham are made available through Jesus Christ and fulfilled in the Holy Spirit. Powerful!

This is my prayer and declaration. I want to see a people that step out of generational curses and into generational blessings. A people who no longer walk in the sins of their fathers, but stand on the shoulders of the greats who have come before us. I want to see the serpent's seed cut off and receive the seed of the woman, the son of David. A people who are not born broken and confused, but are walking in the liberty, fullness, and salvation of Jesus Christ our Lord and Savior. I want to see ungodly soul ties broken and see godly unity established in the body of Christ. I want to see a people who are not mixed up, double minded, and back biting, but who are knit together in heart and spirit. I want to see a people fighting for, defending, and loving one another in unity, working together to extend the kingdom of God.

4 THE BRUISES OF SATAN

I will never forget the first demonic manifestation I witnessed. It was my first semester at Christ for the Nations Institute and the student body was gathered for their morning worship chapel. I remember the worship team was singing about the blood of Jesus and all of a sudden, on the right side of the room, I heard a blood-curling scream. I looked over and a young man whom I did not recognize was lashing out violently to people around him. Some of the instructors encouraged the worship to continue but wanted the young man brought to the altar. Several students grabbed the boy and literally wrestled him and dragged him down to the altar. Hundreds of students, including myself, ran down to the altar excited at the opportunity to cast out a devil!

Even though he was being held on the ground by 8 to 10 people, he had a supernatural strength that made it quite the physical battle. As the students were binding, loosing, and demanding the spirit to come out, I remember hearing the teachers yelling things like "Don't let him bite you!" and "Watch the teeth!" He was foaming at the mouth and trying to get a bite out of a student.

There were times that the demon seemed to leave and the boy would say, "Okay, he's gone." The students would start to let him up only to see demons manifest themselves again as he would begin cursing and trying to run out of the auditorium. The students would again wrestle him to the ground. In retrospect, things were quite chaotic and unorganized. This is not at all how I practice deliverance ministry today, but that's just how this situation happened.

After some time passed with no results one of our instructors, Dr. Carroll Thompson (an elderly man who was in his 70's), had a few able-bodied students usher this young man into a back prayer room. Worship continued and we anxiously waited to see what would happen next. A few minutes later the boy walked out in his right mind, looking like a totally different person. As Dr. Thompson walked out from the back room, I remember some of the students remarking how he was "the exorcist" and things of that nature. All I could think in that moment was, "I want to be used to cast out devils."

Later we found out that young man was not a student but had been invited to attend the morning chapel worship. He ended up enrolling as a student and, in time, shared his testimony. He revealed that God delivered him from various addictions and had broken homosexuality off his life. Satan found an open door in this young man's life, not through generational curse or by sin he allowed in his life, but by a violation of his innocence. He had been sexually abused as a young man. This leads into another way doors can be opened to the oppression of the Devil, the bruises of Satan.

What do I mean by the bruises of Satan? We know the story of the fall. The deceiving serpent, Satan, came to Eve. His influence and temptation led her and her husband to partake of the fruit that God had forbidden. This is the fall of mankind that we are familiar with. What you may not have noticed was the curse that was put upon the serpent in the same chapter of Genesis:

Genesis 3:15 (NKJV)
"and I will put enmity between you and the woman, between your seed and her Seed; He shall bruise your head, and you shall bruise His heel."

From the fall of man, God made it known that there would be warfare and enmity between the seed of the woman, all mankind, and the seed of Satan, his demons, and even unbelievers (who are scripturally referred to as sons of the devil John 8:44). What is enmity? Enmity in the Hebrew is the word *eybah* meaning: hatred, hostility of the mind. Webster's definition of enmity is hatred, animosity, antagonism, hostility. You see a pattern and get the general idea of the meaning. What is interesting is the Greek word for enmity is *echthra*. It adds one other thought to the mix. It means "war." We see the Bible use this word enmity in the New Testament on several occasions

Romans 8:7 (KJV)
"Because the carnal mind is enmity against God: for it is not subject to the law of God, neither indeed can be"

James 4:4 (NKJV)
"Do you not know that friendship with the world is enmity with   God? Whoever therefore wants to be a

friend of the world makes himself an enemy of God."

Consider enmity. The carnal (sinful) mind and friendship with the world are literally hostile toward God. It is creating war between you and God. This brings a new light to these verses. Right after this verse in James, he goes on to say this:

James 4:6 (NKJV)
"God resists the proud, but gives grace to the humble."

It is not just God saying, "I don't like that sin" or "I really wish you would choose to make a better decision." No! God is resisting that sin! God is at war with sin! Since the beginning, there has been a war between good and evil. Whose side are you going to be on?

Consider the other side of things. Maybe you have been cleansed, forgiven, and are walking righteously. The devil is not sitting on the sidelines saying, "I don't like their life of integrity" or "I sure wish they would give into temptation." There is enmity, hatred, and hostility there. Satan wants to antagonize and wage war against your soul.

We have all felt this war on some level. The devil is ruthless. I believe the primary target and prey of the devil is the innocent. He doesn't care if you are a child. The devil will work through a pedophile to defile and bring harm to a child. Satan will kill off a parent or loved one before their time. He will steal your joy and innocence as early as he can. Satan may work through the people you trust the most or in the place that you feel safest. He is hate personified and he has declared war on man, and yes, this includes you. He wants to bruise your soul and leave you hurt and broken.

DESTROYING DEMONIC STRONGHOLDS

2nd Corinthians 10:4-5 (NKJV)
"For the weapons of our warfare are not carnal but mighty in God for pulling down strongholds, casting down arguments and every high thing that exalts itself against the knowledge of God, bringing every thought into captivity to the obedience of Christ."

We have spent so much time blaming things on God that are actually of the devil. Before we look much more into the bruises of Satan, I want us to make sure we recognize the enemy before us.

I remember counseling a young junior high girl who had lost a parent tragically at a young age. They came to me having been deeply bruised and hurt. They were in a place of bitterness and anger that began affecting many areas of their life. We talked through some of the issues and she began to open up about the hurt of losing her father at such a young age. I will never forget one of the questions she asked, "My dad died. Why did God do that?" she asked as she began to weep.

Do you remember what a stronghold is? A wrong belief.

Do you remember what breaks strongholds? Truth!

I looked her dead in the eyes and told her, "God didn't do that." The devil has gained a foothold on the girl. Her dad died in an untimely fashion. Satan came in as the liar that he is, stealing her joy, stealing her peace, and stealing her trust in God. He was speaking lies like, "God did that. God let that happen. God took him."

I believe we get way too theological at times, and if you cannot tell by now, I'm a theologian. We start to look at God's foreknowledge and predestination as a way to reason through the bruises of Satan. Stop! If I were to ask my five-year-old son Gabriel, "Who's the bad guy in the Bible?" I can guarantee you his answer would be "Satan!" I could ask, "Who's the good guy?" He would respond, "Jesus!" "Who hurts us?" "The devil!" "Who heals us?" "God!" "Who makes bad things happen?" "Satan!" "Who makes good things happen?" "Jesus!"

I am not claiming this to be some deep theology, but the enemy has gained a stronghold in too many people that I have met. He has bruised us and deceived us into believing the lie that God is not good. This is a stronghold that can only be broken by the truth of God's word!

Back to the young girl. I remember when I spoke the words, "God didn't do that", she began to weep profusely as the Holy Spirit entered the room and began to minister, bringing her healing and comfort. I asked her, "Do you feel that peace, that comfort, that love? That's God. The abandonment, hatred, and pain you've felt for so long, that's the devil."

These are the bruises of Satan. They can come through the loss of a loved one, abuse, a traumatic event, being fatherless, and even witnessing something terrible. Thankfully, there is healing for the bruises of Satan!

TIME HEALS ALL WOUNDS

One of the most prevalent demonic strongholds is the belief that time heals all wounds. I strongly disagree with that belief. I have ministered to many people, even elderly individuals, who have walked through life emotionally wounded, unable to receive, and seeking sin while being broken, bruised, and bitter. Time has done nothing but allowed hearts to grow hard as unforgiveness and bitterness take root in their lives.

I spent many years with the bruises of Satan that plagued my own life. They came through the hurt of my Dad leaving when I was a very young child. I have no memory of my biological father. I never received the affirmation, value, and love I needed from my father. I struggled with acceptance issues my entire childhood which led me to friendships with drug-using sinners. While I opened the door to so much through willful sin, some of which was generational, the root of nearly all my oppression goes back to the bruises of Satan through fatherlessness.

Maybe you had a father who was physically present but emotionally detached. This can be even more hurtful than having a father who is not there. There is much to be said about the spirit of fatherlessness and the bruising that comes from that spirit. I have an entire section of this book dedicated to the topic.

Satan seeks every opportunity to inflict bruises. Sometimes that can happen through abuse. Maybe you were verbally, sexually, or physically abused or even harassed in school.

Satan has been at war with man. The Bible says that man would bruise his head and he would bruise man's heel, which speaks of this enmity and this war. All who were born after Adam and Eve were considered the seed of the woman. There is good news though. If you were to read Genesis 3:15 (NKJV), you may notice certain capitalized words. It says, "I will put enmity between you and the woman and between your seed and her Seed; He shall bruise your head and you shall bruise His heel." Did you know the Bible capitalizes words that are speaking of Deity? "Seed", "He", and "His" are all speaking of the "man." That means this verse, while speaking of all mankind, is ultimately pointing to the one who would be known as the Second/Last Adam (1 Cor. 15:45-47). The Seed of the Woman is none other than Jesus Christ!

While man has wrestled with Satan and still does, Jesus took the warfare to another level. I love how the original language reads in Genesis 3:15:

Genesis 3:15 (KJV)
"And I will put enmity between thee and the woman and between thy seed and her seed; it shall crush thy head, and thou shall bruise his heel."

This was a prophetic word. We know and have experienced the warfare that followed this curse. This prophetic word spoke of Jesus, the Seed of the Woman, who would crush the head of the serpent! I like to take opportunities to remind the devil where he stands.

OUR DEFEATED FOE

The Bible says that the enemy has been made into Jesus' footstool (Heb 10:13). Not just the devil, but all God's enemies will be made into His footstool (Matthew 22:44). This is not just the position of Jesus Christ who overcame hell, death, and the grave. It is our position too if we are in Christ. We are seated in heavenly places with Him (Eph. 2:6)! Satan may have had authority over you at one time, but the Bible says that every knee must bow at the name of Jesus (Phil 2:10)!

Here is one of my personal favorites (and a personal goal of mine):

> Colossians 2:11,12, 13, 15 (NKJV)
> "In Him you were… buried with Him in baptism, in which you also were raised with Him through faith in the working of God, who raised Him from the dead. And you, being dead in your trespasses and the uncircumcision of your flesh, He has made alive together with Him, having forgiven you all trespasses… Having disarmed principalities and powers, He made a public spectacle of them, triumphing over them…"

My Jesus put Satan and his stooges to open shame! (Feel

free to shout "Hallelujah" right where you are.)

Romans 16:19-20 (ESV)
"But I want you to be wise (excellent) as to what is good and innocent as to what is evil. The God of peace will crush Satan under your feet."

Excellent at good and innocent of evil. This sounds like living holy to me. This sounds like resisting the devil and his wiles and seeing him flee!

Notice what Paul calls God in this passage, "The God of Peace," There is enmity (war, hatred, and animosity) between the devil and man. Do you know what the opposite of war is? Peace! In this war between man and the devil the bruises of Satan will come, but Jesus, the Seed of the Woman, has come to crush the head of Satan! So, if you are excellent at what is good and innocent of evil, you hate bad, and love good, the God of peace will crush Satan under your feet! It doesn't stop there. It's not just that Jesus had some great victory, but as we walk in His victory, freedom, and righteousness that was made available for us, we will see Satan crushed under our feet!

You have been hurt. You have been bruised. You know the devil hates you, and you want to learn to war against him. The first thing you need to know is that you are fighting a defeated foe.

Anderson Silva, at the time of this writing, is an undefeated UFC fighter. Many have marked him as the best fighter in the sport. Can you imagine for a minute being dropped into the hexagon to fist-fight this trained, tested, and victorious fighter? That would be rather frightening. I think there is little question that you would be destroyed. Now let us change the scenario. Someone gets into the ring before you, beats the tar out of Anderson Silva, breaks his limbs, and gives a final blow that literally breaks his skull wide open (sorry if this is too graphic for you), leaving him with a mortal wound. If you were to step into the ring under this scenario, I would say your odds are much better. Even a child would be victorious over this great fighter.

This is said, certainly not to wish harm on Mr. Silva, but to illustrate a point. We have already read the verses about the devil being disarmed, dethroned, crushed, and shamed. The big bad devil who is feared by so many has already been defeated! Jesus did the work!

If reading about what Jesus has already done is not enough, look at Isaiah 14. This is a prophetic passage that speaks about Satan, the antichrist, and his ultimate fall for eternity. I have paraphrased verses 5-17 highlighting my favorite portions:

> "He (Satan) who ruled the people with wrath and unrelenting persecution in anger, but the Lord has broken the staff of the wicked, the whole earth is at peace and quiet and they break into singing.
>
> Sheol, (hell) is stirred up to meet you (Satan), it rouses the dead in hell, kings, rulers, leader, they will say, (Satan) you have become weak as us! Your pomp is brought down to hell, maggots are laid as a bed beneath you, and worms are your covers, oh how you have fallen.

Those who see him will ponder, is this the one who made the earth tremble, who shook kingdoms, who made the world a desert, and overthrew cities?"

You will be joined with the dead in burial. The devil is not a ruler in hell today but a ruler in the world. Fortunately for us, he is a disarmed and disabled ruler who will soon be cast into hell, not as ruler, but judged and damned for eternity.

There is healing for the bruises of Satan. James 5 speaks about healing for our soul. I have included a section in this book called "Restoring - Better Than Before" that gives a walkthrough in how you can seek healing from the bruises of Satan."

5 WHO IN HELL KNOWS YOUR NAME?

Acts 19:11-14 (NKJV)

"Now God worked unusual miracles by the hands of Paul, so that even handkerchiefs and aprons were brought from his body to the sick, and the disease left them and the evil spirits went out from them. Then some of the itinerant Jewish exorcists took it upon themselves to call the name of the Lord Jesus and take over those who had evil spirits, saying, "We exorcise you by the Jesus whom Paul preaches." Also there were seven sons of Sceva, a Jewish chief priest, who did so."

As you have worked through this book, prayerfully you have not only been receiving, but also gaining a desire to walk in this ministry yourself. This chapter is going to deal with some basics on how you can begin to take deliverance to others. "Freely you have received; freely give" (Matthew 10:8).

I love this passage of scripture in Acts. In it Paul was walking in a very powerful anointing. God was working miracles through this man by healing the sick and casting out devils. It said that God worked unusual miracles by the hands of Paul. We serve the same God today! If Paul could be used in power, you can too!

My pastor and mentor, Steve Hill, always encouraged me to plug my name into the Bible. Doing this will help build faith in you. I would read it as, "Now God worked unusual miracles by the hands of Jakob, so that even handkerchiefs or aprons were brought from his body to the sick, and the diseases left them and the evil spirits went out from them." I want you to read that verse and plug your name into it. "Now God worked unusual miracles by the hands of _____, so that even handkerchiefs or aprons were brought from his body to the sick, and the diseases left them and the evil spirits went out from them."

Take a moment to look at your hands and consider the fact that in the same way God used Paul and his hands, He wants to use you and your hands to work miracles, heal diseases, and cast out evil spirits. Before you try and find a demon possessed person to pray for, let us finish this passage and learn from the mistakes of others.

In Acts 19:13, we read about seven brothers, all sons of a Jewish priest whose name was Sceva. The word of Paul's great ministry got around. People were talking about the miracles, his handkerchiefs and aprons, and the healings that were taking place. The thing that stuck with the sons of Sceva was Paul's deliverance ministry. I can imagine one of the brothers telling the story:

"So Paul was preaching and all of a sudden there was a dude who began to manifest demons. It was crazy. I'd seen the guy before he came into the place and he looked pretty crazy from the start. Paul said something about Jesus coming back to life, defeating the devil, and this guy just flipped. It only lasted for a second because Paul just walked right up to the guy and said, 'Go, in Jesus name!', and just like that, the demon went!"

The brothers heard the testimony. They figured since their dad was a pastor, this ministry seemed really simple. There were other Jewish exorcists to follow but Paul's way seemed much easier. So they hit the road in search of a demon possessed fellow. They headed into the home of someone they were pretty sure was demon possessed. They said a little prayer, and sure enough, this guy began to manifest demons. One of the brothers got a jolt of boldness and prayed, "We exorcise you by the Jesus whom Paul preaches." The result of that prayer did not go the way they had thought it would.

Acts 19:15-17 (NKJV)
"And the evil spirit answered and said, "Jesus I know, and Paul I know; but who are you?" Then the man in whom the evil spirit was leaped on them, overpowered them, and prevailed against them, so that they fled out of that house naked and wounded. This became known both to all Jews and Greeks dwelling in Ephesus; and fear fell on them all, and the name of the Lord Jesus was magnified."

I can only imagine what the scene in that house looked like. How violent that demon must have been in order to strip seven men naked? Crazy! I would not wish an experience like that upon anyone! What happened? What went wrong? They used the name of Jesus. They had followed Paul's example. How did things go south so quickly?

Jesus taught a very important lesson in Luke 10 that these pastor's kids would have done well to hear. In Luke 10, Jesus gave seventy disciples authority to heal the sick and cast out devils. In verse 17, they came back rejoicing,

Luke 10:17 (NKJV)
"Then the seventy returned with joy, saying, "Lord, even the demons are subject to us in Your name.""

Jesus was not surprised. He shared that He had seen Satan fall from heaven and He had given the disciples authority and power over the enemy. Then, Jesus expressed something very important.

Luke 10:20 (NKJV)
"Nevertheless do not rejoice in this, that the spirits are subject to you, but rather rejoice because your names are written in heaven."

Jesus quickly reminded them, "You have authority because I gave it to you. Don't rejoice over demons being subject to you, rejoice because you have a relationship with me and you are saved!"

Hear me on this, do not mess with demons if you are not in a relationship with Jesus. This is where the sons of Sceva went wrong. Demons did not have to listen to seven church kids who did not know Jesus. The only power or authority they have is not just in the name of Jesus, but when they are positioned in Him.

The demon replied to the boys in verse 15 saying, "Jesus, I know,"

Know defined in the Greek word is *Ginosko*. It means to learn, to know, come to know, have knowledge of, to become acquainted with, having experiences with.

So, in the original language, that demon said to these boys: "We've had run-ins and experiences with Jesus. We know him well." I'm sure word had gotten around about the ministry of Jesus. They remembered the legion cast into the pigs. They remembered the man who was delivered in the temple and the young epileptic boy. They had encountered Jesus and knew him well. That is not all. The demon said, "Jesus I know (*ginosko*), and Paul I know", but when he spoke of Paul, he did not use the same word *ginosko*, he used the Greek word *epistimi*.

Know defined in the Greek word is *Epistimi*. It means to be acquainted with, to understand, to recognize.

Epistimi is an interesting word. It means to look at something, but remember or think of something else. I am sure there are certain songs that when you hear them you immediately think of something else. A concert you were at or maybe a person you have listened to the song with.

A few years ago I took my family to go Christmas shopping in a city a couple hours away. A few hours into our shopping trip some people in the mall told us that we should probably leave because there were some serious snow storms blowing in. We left and about an hour into our two hour trip the snow started to hit. Wind was blowing hard but the traffic was still going 60-70 miles an hour. I was simply driving with the flow of traffic. Out of nowhere my car began to spin out of control. I hit a patch of black ice. We do a full spin. I can see the lights of semi-trucks and other vehicles coming our way. We do a second spin and start to go off the side of the road. Next thing I know we are flying off the side of the road. We barely miss a guard rail as we go off of the interstate backwards and begin to slide down a steep hill. I was sure we were going to roll down the hill as we were going. The entire car immediately shouted "JESUS" at the top of our lungs. Miraculously our car stayed on all 4 wheels as we flew down this steep hill sideways at 60 mph. Personally, I believe an angel kept us upright. As we came to a stop at the bottom of the hill I turned to my family to make sure everyone was ok. I got out of the car to look around and there wasn't even a scratch on it. No lost hubcaps or anything. Amazing! As I walked around my car I found that we were about 5 feet from a small country road. I turned onto that road, pulled up my GPS, and realized I was on a highway that took me straight to my house.

To this day, every time I drive by that spot on the highway I see that guard rail, that patch of road, the steep hill, and the little road at the bottom and remember how the Lord preserved us that night. If I took you to that spot, all you would see is a spot on the highway. When I look at it, I remember the miracle that took place there.

This is an example of *epistimi*. When the demons in this man saw Paul, they immediately saw Jesus in him. Most would look at Paul and just see a man, but these demons saw Paul and they recognized the same Spirit, the same power, the same authority that was in Jesus. I see Paul, but I remember Jesus! Paul had a relationship with Jesus, He had put on Christ, and Christ was in Him!

Now consider how this demon responded, "Jesus I know (*ginosko*, we've had run-ins, and encounters with), and Paul I know (*epistimi*, we are acquainted with him, we have seen Christ in Him); but who are you?" No deep meaning in that last part. This demon spirit recognized that these boys had no right or authority over them and no position in Christ. He proceeded to jump them, overpower them, beat them, strip them, and at the end of this sad story, we see these seven brothers running nude down the road humiliated.

I had a friend who shared a similar story. For the sake of privacy, I will call him Phillip. Phillip grew up in a good, spirit-filled church that was not unfamiliar with the demonic. In one church service, a woman began to manifest demons and many of the members of the church gathered around to pray. Figuring it was the right thing to do, Phillip joined the circle and began praying the spirit would come out of the woman. The problem with this was Phillip was living in blatant sin and had no active relationship with Jesus. As everyone was praying, this demon looked at Phillip and said, "You don't have the authority or position to command me. You look at pornography and masturbate and you don't have the right!"

This is why you have to be in right standing with Jesus to take authority over demonic powers! This is also why we need to seek free people to pray freedom into our lives. I have a section in this book about restoration and the need to seek out righteous people to whom we can confess our sins and from whom we can receive prayer. Take it from Sceva's sons and from my friend Phillip.

YOU HAVE AUTHORITY!

If you are in a right relationship with Jesus, you have great authority! The problem with many Christians is that we can say we are Christian, but we do not recognize the power of the Holy Spirit in us! You know that the devil is not going to show up and tell you, "Oh, by the way, you have authority over me. You're stronger than me." The devil wants to blind us to this fact! I am sure the devil would love to re-enact Acts 19 and beat you, strip you down, and humiliate you. Do not let the devil tell you who you are! Let the Word of God tell you who you are!

1st John 4:4 (KJV)
"Greater is he that is in you, than he that is in the world."

The devil will revel in our ignorance. This is why I feel like the deliverance message is so important. I pray you will help spread this message of freedom! When you know the truth, it will make you free. (John 8:32)

Matthew 16:19
"And I will give unto thee the keys of the kingdom of heaven: and whatsoever thou shalt bind on earth shall be bound in heaven: and whatsoever thou shalt loose on earth shall be loosed in heaven."

Keys are symbols of authority. "Keys" here is the Greek word is *klice*, meaning the ability to open a locked door or shut and lock an open door. You can not clean a house if you do not have access to it. These keys are to bind Satan and loose captives, to close the door and lock Satan out of the house, and to open the door of freedom for captives locked away. "Binding and loosing" have to do with "forbidding and permitting!" We bind Satan by forbidding the demons control and commanding their departure. We loose people by permitting them to walk free by the power of Jesus' name and by His Word.

During one of the first demonic manifestations that I ever witnessed, this young man balled up his fist and was coming at me full force with every intention of punching me in the face. I didn't contemplate my theology in that moment. The Spirit of God came over me and the words just left my mouth, "I BIND YOU IN THE NAME OF JESUS!" I wish I had a recording of what happened next. I watched as if God Himself took that demon-possessed man's arm by the wrist and firmly brought it to the side of his body. Thankfully, I didn't get punched and I saw the spoken word of prayer bring forth immediate results.

What are these keys Jesus is speaking of in Matthew 16? While there are possibly several keys, I want to encourage you to study out and pray on two specifically. These keys are the two most powerful tools God gave to His church, the name of Jesus and His infallible Word!

Revelation 12:11 talks about overcoming the devil by the blood of the Lamb and the word of your testimony.

The blood and the Word.

These keys are wielded and used by your spirit in agreement with and in the power of the Holy Spirit. If you want to do business with heaven, Jesus' name and His Word are the keys in order to do that.

6 The Blood of Jesus

The blood of Jesus is so powerful! The same way that demons looked at Paul and recognized Jesus in and on him, demons can look at you the same way! If you've been washed and redeemed by the blood of Jesus you have the same devil driving authority that he operated in.

Several years ago I was working with a mission's organization in Honduras building homes for those who didn't have. We had brought all the necessary tools and wheeled them up to the location where we would soon begin to dig a trench to lay the foundation. We dropped off the tools and broke briefly for lunch. Some of the locals were anxious to begin work so they started while we were at break. When we returned we saw a humorous sight. The Hondurans were digging out the trench with machetes, throwing the dirt into the wheelbarrow by hand, and then began scooping the dirt out with the shovels we had left there. They didn't realize that the shovels could be used to break the ground and scoop the dirt or that the dirt could be dumped right out of the wheelbarrow. They were making their job so much harder simply because they didn't realize the tools that they had at their exposure and hadn't been taught how to use them properly.

I meet believers all the time that have no idea that Jesus shed His blood to benefit us in so many ways. For instance, we can access healing, deliverance, liberty in our mind and so much more. We may find healing or soundness in mind in a way that gets the job done. Most do not realize that the word of God outlines a set of tools and weapons that we can utilize that will make our life much easier!

God has always associated freedom and forgiveness with the shedding of blood. In Leviticus 17:11 and Exodus 24 we see the priests and Moses sprinkling blood for the forgiveness of sin. This is a theme that is carried throughout the New Testament as well.

Hebrews 9:22 (NKJV)
"And according to the law almost all things are purified with blood, and without shedding of blood there is no remission."

Matthew 26:28 (KJV)
"For this is my blood of the new testament, which is shed for many for the remission of sins."

Beyond forgiveness, Jesus shed His blood to cover many areas of our life. If you walk through the story of the crucifixion and the events leading up to it, you will see several times that Jesus shed His blood. Each of these carries significance and power for us today.

Jesus Shed Blood On His Face

Luke 22:41-44 (KJV)
"And he was withdrawn from them about a stone's cast, and kneeled down, and prayed, Saying, Father, if thou be willing, remove this cup from me: nevertheless not my will, but thine, be done. And there appeared an angel unto him from heaven, strengthening him. And being in an agony he prayed more earnestly: and his sweat was as it were great drops of blood falling down to the ground."

This is the blood that covers our oppression.

You may not know but there is an actual condition called hematidrosis where individuals under intense mental agony or stress actually sweat blood. When people experience incredible mental pressure the pores become so dilated that blood may actually spill from them.

Jesus, here in the garden of Gethsemane, knew that He was facing a bitter cup. He knew He was to carry the weight of the sin of all humanity. As He was now nearing that brutal death, He began to see and smell what was in that cup.

Jesus was beginning to take on the mental oppression that you and I would face. He was about to undergo the anguish of mind, anxiety, fear, and insecurity. Jesus shed His blood in the midst of the greatest mental anguish one could face. In doing so, He has covered over the anguish that would come upon us.

As we come under the blood of Jesus, we also come into the victory that He had over this anguish. Until you literally have the weight of the sin of the world on your mind, you can rest assured that Jesus has endured more and He is willing and able to share that victory with you!

My wife is a great example of this. There was a fear and anxiety that surrounded her in many areas. While we were dating and going through Bible College, I was very active in ministry. I would preach and teach often and would minister on prayer teams. My heart's desire from day one was that my wife and I would minister alongside one another in all we did. The problem was that she was afraid to pray out loud much less in the altars over other people. She even had a fear of reading her Bible out loud out of a fear that she would sound dumb.

You may relate to this, and it may not seem like a big deal, but when you're getting ready to transition into full time ministry and you're wondering if your soon-to-be spouse will participate with you in what you feel is your life calling, it's a big deal!

I'll never forget one night we were in a church service where a guest minister was in the house. We had actually been fighting before the service because I was asked to be ready to minister in the altars if the guest speaker asked for a prayer team. Being newly engaged, the pastor of the church had asked if Leah would minister with me. I said yes. She, on the drive to the church, said "no."

There I am ministering in the altars, alone, when the guest speaker gets a hold of my fiancé. I watched him lay hands on her and the power of God hit her in a way that I have seen very few other times. It was like lightning went through her body. She shot back a good five feet from the minister and shook on the ground. After the service I asked her what had happened. She, still shaking, began to share that when she hit the ground she felt as if God was literally burning away fear that had come upon her so often. She knew she could pray out now, read her Bible, and more. I, being the gracious man that I am, said, "Prove it. Pray for me right now." Sure enough she prayed for me, our marriage, and our ministry. Powerful! It was the first time I'd heard her pray out loud.

Jesus is saying, "I drank that cup for you!" That fear and anxiety that can grip and paralyze our mind, Jesus not only endured it, but He overcame it! Due to Him shedding His blood, He has also covered over our minds and that victory is ours as well.

Jesus Shed Blood Shed On His Back

Isaiah 53:5 (KJV)
"But he was wounded for our transgressions, he was bruised for our iniquities: the chastisement of our peace was upon him; and with his stripes we are healed."

1st Peter 2:22-24 (KJV)
"Who did no sin, neither was guile found in his mouth: Who, when he was reviled, reviled not again; when he suffered, he threatened not; but committed himself to him that judgeth righteously: Who his own self bare our sins in his own body on the tree, that we, being dead to sins, should live unto righteousness: by whose stripes ye were healed."

The blood shed on Jesus' back covers our physical healing. This book isn't about physical healing nearly as much as it's about spiritual/soul healing. That being said, you can rest in confidence that Jesus is healer. The same way we can trust Him to move in our emotions and heal our soul; we can trust Him for physical healing as well. He allowed His back to be beaten with a horrible whip so that we could be healed. He suffered a beating that would have killed many men. While He was enduring the scourging and whipping, He was shedding His blood. Again, Jesus was victorious even over physical abuse. When He appeared to His disciples He didn't appear with open wounds, but with scars. His blood has been made available to us, meaning His victory over the physical body is available as well.

I've seen many healing's throughout our years of ministry including: Tumors falling off, heart issues resolved, and even a woman who was wheelchair bound for 15 years standing up to walk! So many powerful demonstrations of the healing power of God through the shed blood of Jesus.

One thing that I have never seen healed was a scar. I believe this is for a couple reasons. Jesus, even after His healing and resurrection, still bore His scars. Our scars tell a story! They are a mark of a healed wound. I can observe scars all over my body and consider what the Lord has brought me through.

Jesus Shed Blood On His Head

Matthew 27:28-30 (KJV)
"And they stripped him, and put on him a scarlet robe.

And when they had platted a crown of thorns, they put it upon his head, and a reed in his right hand: and they bowed the knee before him, and mocked him, saying, Hail, King of the Jews! And they spit upon him, and took the reed, and smote him on the head."

The blood Jesus shed on His Head covers our psychological and emotional struggles.

As Jesus was receiving this twisted crown of thorns, He was mocked and insulted. As these soldiers were abusing Him physically and emotionally, He was spilling blood from His head.

For this reason I refuse to allow verbal or physical abuse to grip my mind. I don't believe we need to accept a diagnosis of depression, bi-polar disorder, or A.D.D. If Jesus shed blood to cover our mind, we ought to stand for freedom and liberty in our mind as well. This isn't to say that God will brainwash you of all the hurt you've ever experienced. Scars, we all bear them. Jesus overcame this abuse and accomplished His mission, shedding blood, so that we could share in His victory. We don't need to be paralyzed or broken in our emotions even if we have suffered verbal or physical abuse and mockery.

The same way God can heal a physical body, He can heal a mind. I've seen amazing work and victory come in the mind of other individuals.

I have a close friend who served several tours in the Middle East as a Sergeant in the Army. His vehicles had been blown up several times and he was honorably discharged because of the physical injuries he had sustained. When I met "Sarge" he was limping around with a cane. I didn't know that he had been previously wheelchair bound. The Lord had done a tremendous healing work in his physical body. Today he walks with no cane, dances in worship, and even works overseas in missions.

While the physical work was powerful, Sarge struggled greatly with post-traumatic stress disorder. There were times that worship would get loud or he would get caught in a crowd and would have flashbacks to some of the horrors of war he had suffered. It wasn't too long into his pursuit of the Lord that he heard that the same way God had healed his physical body; He could heal his mind as well.

Unlike some other cases, I can't say that it was one powerful moment in prayer or at an altar that PTSD was broken, but Sarge walked by faith continually claiming the victory that is in the shed blood of Jesus. Today he can be in a service or in a crowd and no longer have episodes or flashbacks. He sleeps in peace with no nightmares and can effectively testify that Jesus has taken that PTSD and restored his mind.

That's the power of the shed blood of Jesus!

Jesus Shed Blood On His Hands

Matthew 27:35 (KJV)
"And they crucified him, and parted his garments, casting lots: that it might be fulfilled which was spoken by the prophet, They parted my garments among them, and upon my vesture did they cast lots."

I'm so thankful that Jesus shed His blood for us. I'm very thankful that His hands, which had never done a sinful thing, bled to cover my hands which have worked many wicked things.

Psalm 24:3-4 (KJV)
"Who shall ascend into the hill of the LORD? or who shall stand in his holy place? He that hath clean hands, and a pure heart; who hath not lifted up his soul unto vanity, nor sworn deceitfully."

I can't tell you how many times I've heard people talk about how good their hearts are when they are seeking to justify themselves. Individuals feeling guilty over their lack of faith or their pursuit of God in prayer quickly turn to a statement like, "God looks at the heart" or "God sees my heart."

That may be true! I would say that I've got a pretty good heart. Even when I was far from God and deep in sin I still had compassion for people and cared for their general well-being. In fact, I went on a few mission trips with a church because I cared enough about people suffering in third world countries to try and do something about it. Good heart.

Unfortunately, that verse in Psalms talks about two major prerequisites to drawing near to the Lord. It's not just a matter of a good or pure heart, but it also deals with clean hands!

We have already touched on repentance in previous chapters but don't ever forget that the reason we can even be washed clean is because Jesus shed His blood! His sinless hands were pierced and blood was shed to cover our sinful hands. This is the only way we can have "clean hands."

The blood shed from Jesus' hands covers every work that our hands have done and will do. Hands that once participated in sin can now be used for God's glory. Hands that were once fighting and abusive can now lay hands on the sick and see them recover. Hands that once gratified the flesh can now be lifted in reverential worship to our Lord. Hands that have held beer bottles and illegal drugs now turn the pages of a Bible.

Another thing to note is that all throughout scripture God highlights hands. Specifically, His right hand as a hand of authority.

As Jesus shed His blood and we come underneath it, we get to share in His authority.

Luke 11:20 (NKJV)
"But if I cast out demons with the finger of God, surely the kingdom of God has come upon you."

This is a powerful verse that marked a new season. You can witness demonic activity in the Old Testament. In 1st Samuel 16 you can read about King Saul being tormented by demonic spirits. David would play the harp and pacify the demons but didn't have the authority to cast them out. In fact, you will never see anyone in the Old Testament casting out demons. This is why people were so astonished with the ministry of Jesus. Jesus didn't come to pacify devils; He came to cast them out!

In Luke 11, Jesus gives us an illustration. You have a strong man guarding a kingdom. It's going to take a stronger man to overtake that man to gain access to the kingdom. Jesus is the stronger man! We may have had demonic activity operating within the abode of a man but Jesus came and with His hand of authority drove the demons out!

The fact that Jesus shed blood on His hands and has covered ours gives us the ability to walk in that authority over the demonic. If you've come to repentance then you've been washed and cleansed by the blood of Jesus and now you can stand in authority and resist the devil. He must flee!

Jesus Shed Blood On His Feet

Along the same line of thinking, Jesus shed blood from his feet to cover everywhere you have been or will go.

Proverbs 1:15-16 (KJV)
"My son, walk not thou in the way with them; refrain thy foot from their path: For their feet run to evil, and make haste to shed blood."

Our feet used to run to evil. We have run into the bars or into the room where adultery would be committed. We have run to participate in a fight or run blatantly away from the will of God.

Jesus shed His blood to cover every step you have taken. His feet that had never once strayed from the narrow, hard path that His Father had laid out before Him were pierced to cover our feet that have so often gone astray.

There are so many times that I have missed God. At times I felt that I should go and pray for someone, but out of pride or fear, walked the other way. There are times that I should have walked to help someone in need, but out of laziness or selfishness, went the other direction. Thank God that He covers every stray step we've taken.

I often compare God's will to a GPS. God has a plan for our life. He has an end goal and a purpose for every one of us. When I type in a location to my GPS I know where I want to end up. As I start to drive there are many things that can happen. I could get distracted and miss a turn. There may be construction or an accident that slows me down or takes me off track. The wonderful thing about a GPS is that when you get off track you will hear it quickly announce, "Re-routing!" If you continue to follow the device, assuming it's working correctly, you will eventually arrive at your destination.

This isn't entirely different from the way God can work in our lives. He has a purpose and destiny for our lives. Very often we miss turns, go off track, or even have accidents that slow us down. God has a way of re-routing us and getting us back on track. Through restoration, our straying can even become a testimony of God's goodness and faithfulness. It can serve as an encouragement to others who have gone astray. If we are mindful of the path God is laying out before us, we will arrive at God's desired destination for our lives.

Jesus Shed Blood From His Side

John 19:32-34 (KJV)
"Then came the soldiers, and brake the legs of the first,

and of the other which was crucified with him. But when they came to Jesus, and saw that He was dead already, they brake not his legs: But one of the soldiers with a spear pierced his side, and forthwith came there out blood and water."

The blood shed from the side of Jesus covers everything that is close to our heart. There is a lot that could be said on this one point but I'll save that for another book.

This was a powerful moment. Jesus, because of His amazing love for us had finished the work. The soldiers pierced His side to confirm that He had died. Blood and water came forth from His side.

The blood speaks of forgiveness and washing of our sins. The water can symbolize the ongoing work of sanctification by the washing of the Word and the work of the Holy Spirit.

Consider the parallel, as Adam's side was opened his bride, Eve, was created. As Jesus' side was opened, His blood was spilled which created the means through which His bride, the church, could be received to Himself.

This is our salvation! This is the accomplished work of Jesus Christ. This is not only something that we stepped into the day we believed and received it, but it's also a promise for the future. Still to this day, the bride is being made ready for the return of Jesus. Deliverance plays a major part in preparing the bride! Jesus is serious enough about spending eternity with you that He died for you! If that was all He ever did, it would be enough. Jesus suffered much and shed His blood in many ways so that even in this life we could step into freedom, healing, and sound-mindedness. Today this is available to all!

7 FATHERLESSNESS

Chapter 6 deals with the bruises of Satan that can come through our relationships with our fathers and mothers. This is quite possibly the most significant and common place where the bruises of Satan enter. My heart is not for you to walk away thinking you have daddy issues, but to give you some scripture and guide you in prayer to release hurts that may be there. I want you to get on the path to healing the bruises of Satan that came through these issues.

In his book *Experiencing the Fathers Embrace* (which is an excellent read), Jack Frost outlines several father figures we may have had in our life. I am sure one or more will be fitting in your life.

The Good Father

Some have grown up with such a good father that they may have problems letting go of that earthly figure and trusting entirely on God. Daughters may find it difficult to

97

leave and cleave when the time comes because they compare their spouse with the characteristics of their father. Beyond this, our fathers shape the way we view our heavenly father. Our fathers may have been considered good fathers, but they were far from perfect. As good as they may have been, they are not as good as God. Even good fathers let us down, disappoint us, and unfortunately, are not around forever.

The Performance Oriented Father

It's very common in American society to reward individuals who perform successfully whether it be in sports, careers, academics, or the financial market. You may have heard your earthly father say that he loved you but that was only after you measured up to his high expectations. This can cause us to see God in the same light. God will only love us if we read our Bible enough and pray enough.

While boundaries and standards are a great thing to have, we need to gain an understanding of God's perfect love. Any correction is not about your performance, but comes entirely from the place of deep love for you. Prayer and time in the Word is not about gaining God's approval, but spending time with our Abba (daddy). He loves you and simply wants to be with his child!

The Passive Father

This type of father does not reject his children, but also doesn't place any great demands on them either. He simply fails to be at home, even when he is at home. He rarely demonstrates love or affection, probably because he never received these things either. This is very common in workaholic fathers. This can cause us to look at God in the same way. Our relationship with God is empty of passion and joy. It's all about discipline, form, duty, and no emotion! We give God mental and intellectual ascent but don't open up our heart to him.

The Absentee Father

This is the father that is not present. He has either died or is not involved in the children's life. The latter is the case for nearly 50% of American children. Even if they have a great stepfather, many of these children will have abandonment issues. They may feel that God is not always there for them. This may push them to strive to please God because they feel guilty for their father leaving. Hebrews 13:5 says our Father will never leave or forsake us.

The Authoritarian Father

This goes far beyond the performance-oriented father. There is a stern demand for immediate, unquestioned obedience from the children. Little emotion other than fear, intimidation, and control are expressed. God is seen as a harsh authoritarian figure to be feared and obeyed rather than a loving father one would want to love and cherish.

The Abusive Father

Verbal, emotional, physical, and sexual abuse is becoming more and more common in families throughout the United States. If you have been abused in any of these ways, often times you need more than counseling or psychological help to be free of deep pain and anger.

Abuse, especially sexual abuse, creates one of the deepest wounds a child can ever receive. It can violate the trust the child has placed in authority and can affect all their relationships for the rest of their lives. They will have a hard time fully trusting God, a pastor, or other authority figures. It can create feelings of guilt, shame, unworthiness, or that they did something to deserve being treated so badly. We need healing that can only come through the Holy Spirit pouring the love of God into our heart.

Romans 5:5
"This hope never disappoints or deludes or shames us, for God's love has been poured out in our hearts through the Holy Spirit who was given to us."

WHAT IS REQUIRED OF US FOR HEALING?

Psalm 45:10-11 (NASB)

"Listen, o daughter, give attention and incline your ear; forget your people and your father's house; then the King will desire your beauty; because He is your Lord, bow down to Him."

What is required? To give your earthly father the gift that he may not deserve, forgiveness.

We have to be willing to forgive our fathers in the areas they failed to represent the love of Father God to us. If we do not forgive, we may end up carrying the baggage of father issues for much of our life. You do not want to find your identity in the pain and disappointments of your earthly father's house!

Hurt people, hurt people. Your father probably gave all he knew to give. Placing blame on our fathers for our problems can increase our troubles and the sense of separation from God. While you may have been innocent of the wounding you received in your father's house, you are accountable for the dishonor (disrespect) you display towards your father.

Healing can begin when you start to forgive, take personal responsibility for present issues, and stop seeking to blame others for them. You may not have ever received blessings or love, but God wants to give you what you have lacked today!

Here are some verses to meditate on and declare over yourself:

1 John 3:1 (NKJV)
"Behold what manner of love the Father has bestowed on us, that we should be called children of God!"

Hosea 14:3-4
"For my father and my mother have forsaken me, but the lord will take me up (Ps. 27:10)... a father of the fatherless... god makes a home for the lonely; he leads out the prisoners into prosperity (Ps. 68:5-6)... for in thee the orphan finds mercy. I will heal their apostasy; I will love them freely."

John 14:18,21,23; 16:27).
"I will not leave you as orphans; I will come to you... he who has my commandments and keeps then, it is he who loves me; and he who loves me shall be loved by my father, and I will love him, and will disclose myself to him... if anyone loves me, he will keep my word; and my father will love him, and we will come to him and make our abode with him... for the father himself loves you, because you have loved me, and have believed that I came forth from the father."

Next, I would encourage you to take time to pray and choose to forgive your father for each way he hurt or disappointed you. Be specific! This may take some time but the Holy Spirit will lead you. You may find it helpful to make a list or to get with a pastor or an accountability partner to pray with you or lead you in prayer.

THE MOTHER LOVE OF
THE FATHER GOD

There have been many sermons preached and books written that minister to fatherlessness and the bruises that have come. There has been far less dealing with mother issues. It is true that there are far more who are fatherless than motherless, but as shown in the last section, much of that hurt and bruising can come even if the father is present.

Many have heard of the various types of love in the Bible, *agape*, *phileo*, and *eros*. There is also a rarely taught Greek word for love that is found in the Bible called *storge* love. This is a family love that speaks of nurturing, empathy, affection, and tenderness to one another.

Even in the animal kingdom, it's the mothers who are the primary caregivers during the first years of life. It's very much the same with us. The mother's *storge* love imparts faith in the child to bond, receive, and express love. You probably don't remember this, but your relationship with your mother was your first experience with expressed love. This time is vital to forming the way you feel about yourself, the world, and God.

Psalm 22:9-10 (NKJV)

"But You (God) are He who took me out of the womb; you made me trust while on my mother's breasts. I was cast upon You from birth. From my mother's womb You have been my God."

You may not have received *storge* love from your mom or dad. You may not have experienced that affectionate touch, eye contact, or a loving tone of voice. You may know that you struggle offering the same love to others. God wants to love you with this *storge* love so you can, in turn, love others with this same love.

WHAT IS REQUIRED OF US FOR HEALING?

First, we cannot take a victim mentality even if we were physically or emotionally wounded. While these things may have happened apart from our own actions, we made a choice somewhere along the lines to shut ourselves out and look to false loves or ungodly affections. God wants you to experience His *storge* love today. He longs for you to choose to love Him no matter how you have been violated or failed in the past.

Babies do not have to do anything to be loved, they just receive it! Maybe you have never received *storge* love from your mother and there is a longing in your heart. Your mother may have forgotten or abandoned you, but God never has. No matter what type of mother you may have had and how deeply you may have been hurt, God's unconditional love will always remember you.

Isaiah 49:15-16 (NKJV)
"Can a woman forget her nursing child, and not have compassion on the son of her womb? Surely they may forget, yet I will not forget you. See I have inscribed you on the palms of My hands."

God wants to offer the same love of a mother to you today!

Isaiah 66:11-13 (NKJV)
"That you may feed and be satisfied with the consolation of her bosom, that you may drink deeply and be delighted with the abundance of her glory. For thus says the Lord: behold I will extend peace to her like a river and the glory of the gentiles like a flowing stream then you shall feed; on her sides shall you be carried, and be fondled on her knees. As one whom his mother comforts, so I will comfort you; and you shall be comforted in Jerusalem"

Take time to meditate on these verses that express God's love for you.

Jeremiah 31:3; 1:5
"I have loved you with an everlasting love; therefore I have drawn you with loving-kindness... Before I formed you in the womb I knew you, and before you were born I consecrated you"

Psalm 139:13,17-18; 71:6
"For you formed my inward parts; you weaved me in my mother's womb, how precious are thy thoughts to me, O God! How vast is the sum of them! If I should count them, they would outnumber the sand. By thee, I have been sustained from my birth; you are him who took me from my mother's womb; my praise is continually of you!"

Psalm 22:9-10

"Yet you are Him who brought me from the womb; you made me trust when upon my mother's breast, upon you I was cast from birth, you have been my God from my mother's womb"

Though you may feel emotionally rejected, abandoned, or orphaned by your parents, God does not want to leave you in this condition. Even if you feel too wounded to come to Him, He will come to you. He will not leave you like an orphan.

For my father and mother have forsaken me, but the Lord will take me up – He is the Father to the fatherless. God makes a home for the lonely. I will not leave you as orphans; I will come to you.

I would encourage you to take some of the verses that I have listed here and in the previous chapter and declare the Word of God over your life! Be intentional about speaking out your forgiveness to your mother or father. This is essential for healing and restoration to come! As you speak that out, ask the Lord to minister His love and heart to you!

8 RESTORING, BETTER THAN BEFORE!

Psalm 51:12 (NKJV)
"Restore to me the joy of Your salvation and uphold my innocence by Your generous Spirit."

Many know that the word "restore" means to "put it back", but that isn't the full extent of the meaning. Restoration has a full definition which is "to put it back better than it was before!" When something is restored in scripture, it's always increased, multiplied, or improved so that its latter state is significantly better than its original state. By now, I am sure the Holy Spirit has begun to highlight some areas in your life that need attention. James shares about restoration and spiritual healing:

James 5:16 (NKJV)
"Confess your trespasses to one another, and pray for one another, that you may be healed. The effective, fervent prayer of a righteous man avails much."

Some may wonder why they actually need to go to someone else for prayer. While forgiveness is something that can happen between you and God, spiritual healing often times needs to take place through confession and prayer.

Healed in the Greek language is *Iaomia* which is defined as, to cure, heal, to make whole, to free from errors and sins, to bring about (one's) salvation.

This is talking about soul healing and freedom from sin. When the Bible speaks about physical healing, it uses the Greek word *sozo*.

James is outlining how to receive healing and deliverance!

Hopefully by now, you are thinking "Enough with the Greek, I'm ready to have all ties broken and be free!"

1. Confession – You need to be specific with God. The enemy gained a foothold through a specific sin that you have committed. You need to be specific about the sin you need Jesus to forgive (no prayers like "God forgive me for everything I've ever done").

You might make a list of areas in which you feel you need deliverance. Take time and pray that the Holy Spirit reveals to your heart every area of oppression, every generational curse, and every area of hurt that needs healed.

2. Repentance – This is very important! If you are actively sinning, repentance needs to take place. To repent means to change your mind and to turn away. Stop the sin! If you are set free from any demonic issue and choose to indulge in that

sin again, even in the mind, you open the door to the same stronghold, seven times stronger!

Matthew 12:43-45 (NKJV)
"When an unclean spirit goes out of a man, he goes through dry places, seeking rest, and finds none. Then he says, 'I will return to the house from which I came.' And when he comes, he finds it empty, swept, and put in order. Then he goes and takes with him seven other spirits more wicked than himself, and they enter and dwell there; and the last state of that man is worse than the first."

I cannot stress the importance of this 2nd point. Deliverance is not something that you seek because your small group, your spouse, or anyone else is pushing you to it. You need to know that you are done with the sin you have been living in. I knew a young woman who went through a very powerful time of deliverance and within a week, was back in the same sin. Within weeks, her marriage had fallen apart, she was in deeper addiction and immorality than ever before, and she began having mental issues.

3. Have a righteous man or woman pray with you. You need to seek out a person who is walking in freedom. This is the Biblical outline. You have given the enemy a legal right to oppress you. As we have established already, he does not have to go because you do not have authority over him due to you being bound in sin. Go to someone who has received freedom who can legally take authority over the enemy.

4. Believe that the work has been done! This is a step of faith. You have to believe and be ready to receive freedom

and total healing from the past.

5. Fill the gap! After something has either been cast out or swept clean, you need to make sure you fill that space with God! Especially the first few weeks! Make sure you are filling yourself up with the Word, prayer, worship, and godly fellowship.

6. Be ready for the return but do not receive it! As the above Matthew text says, it is very possible that the spirit that has been broken off or cast out will try and come back to see if someone (God) is dwelling in his old room. Recognize your enemy, but stand in faith that not only have you been forgiven, but you have also been healed and set free!

9 SCRIPTURES FOR VICTORY

Our greatest tool in resisting the devil is the Word of God. Take and pray these verses over your life!

Rom 6:1-3 What shall we say then? Shall we continue in sin, that grace may abound? God forbid. How shall we, that are <u>dead to sin</u>, live any longer therein? Know ye not, that so many of us as were baptized into Jesus Christ were <u>baptized into his death</u>?

Rom 6:7 For he that is dead is freed from sin.

Rom 6:14 For <u>sin shall not have dominion over you</u>: for ye are not under the law, but under grace.

Rom 8:1-2 There is therefore now no condemnation to them which are in Christ Jesus, who walk not after the flesh, but after the Spirit. For the law of the Spirit of life in Christ Jesus hath <u>made me free from the law of sin and death</u>.

Eph 2:10 For we are his workmanship, created in Christ

Jesus unto <u>good works</u>, which God hath before ordained that we should walk in them.

Mat 1:21 And she shall bring forth a son, and thou shalt call his name JESUS: for he <u>shall save his people *from* their sins.</u>

Luke 4:18 The Spirit of the Lord is upon me, because he hath anointed me to preach the gospel to the poor; he hath sent me to <u>heal the brokenhearted</u>, to <u>preach deliverance to the captives</u>, and recovering of sight to the blind, to set at <u>liberty them that are bruised,</u>

Mat 10:8 Heal the sick, cleanse the lepers, raise the dead, <u>cast out devils: freely ye have received, freely give.</u>

Heb 12:1 let us lay aside every weight, and the sin which doth so easily beset us, and let us run with patience the race that is set before us,

1Jo 2:16 For all that is in the world, the lust of the flesh, and the lust of the eyes, and the pride of life, is not of the Father, but is of the world.

1Jo 5:4 For whatsoever is born of God overcometh the world: and this is the <u>victory that overcometh the world</u>, even our faith.

1Co 10:13 There hath <u>no temptation taken you</u> but such as is common to man: but God is faithful, who will not suffer you to be tempted above that ye are able; but will with the temptation also make a way to escape, that ye may be able to bear it.

2Co 5:21 For he hath made him to be sin for us, who knew no sin; that <u>we might be made the righteousness of God in Him.</u>

Jam 4:7 Submit yourselves therefore to God. <u>Resist the devil, and he will flee from you.</u>

Made in the USA
Middletown, DE
04 July 2023